THE BOOK OF DECORATIVE KNOTS

For Becky Owen

· THE BOOK OF ·
DECORATIVE KNOTS

PETER OWEN

Lyons & Burford, Publishers

Design and Illustration by Peter Owen.

Printed in the United States of America

10 9 8 7 6 5

Library of Congress Cataloging-in-Publication Data

Owen, Peter, 1950-
    The book of decorative knots : complete instructions for over 60 functional and beautiful knots – for home, camp, and more – / Peter Owen.

    p. cm.
    ISBN 1-55821-304-X

    1. Macramé. 2. Ropework. 3. Knots and splices. I. Title.
    II. Title: Decorative knots.
TT840.M33094 1994
746.42'2–dc20

                                                                94-5176
                                                                CIP

CONTENTS

· · · · · · · · · · · · · · · ·

· · · · · · · · · · · · · · · ·

INTRODUCTION

D ecorative or "Fancy" knots and knot work have held in the past, as they do today, a particular fascination in the way they combine what is useful with the aesthetically pleasing. Few knots included in this category are purely decorative. Most have practical applications and are derived from or based on well known standard knots, but they all allow for individual creativity through personal ingenuity and inventiveness and, in the complexity and precision of their formation, can be as absorbing and satisfying as any puzzle.

Decorative knotting has a long and distinguished history and is one of the oldest and most widely distributed of the folk arts. It is still widely practised. Over the years, it has retained wide popular appeal and fascination, and now has the status of a recognized art form.

In the past, the intricacies of knot formation could take a long time to acquire; the knowledge being passed on from one individual to another, often under pledge of secrecy. *The Book of Decorative Knots* gives you the opportunity, through clear instructions and easy to follow step-by-step illustrations, to master 50 classic decorative knots within a few hours. The knots, meticulously explained and described, are not just decorative and attractive in their own right, but have a multitude of modern applications in all walks of life as well – from sailing, fishing, hunting and outdoorsmanship, to the worlds of fashion and interior design.

HISTORY

The art of knotting is as ancient as humankind. Stone Age peoples used knots to secure and fasten their traps, clothing and housing; coiled and braided rope was found in the tomb of Tutankhamun; the Inca people of Peru used knotted string instead of written figures and the Greeks, Romans, and other ancient civilizations probably knew as much about knots as we do today.

Throughout this long history, the decorative potential of the knot has been almost as important as its practical function. This aspect of knot making can be found in many places and many ages, from the elaborate patterning on Celtic artifacts to the fringe on the gown of Leonardo da Vinci's Mona Lisa. It was, however, seamen and sailors, particularly those who served aboard the great sailing vessels of the eighteenth and nineteenth centuries, who made decorative knot tying a branch of folk art peculiarly their own.

The length of the voyages undertaken by sailing ships left sailors with little to do for much of the time; this was particularly true on whalers which were at sea longer than other ships and were heavily overmanned. Isolated on board, unable for the most part to read and write, sailors had to find some way to fill their idle hours and knotting was an ideal way of passing the time.

There was no shortage of raw materials. Sailing ships carried miles of rigging, and there was always a plentiful supply of spoiled rope (known as "junk") available for knotting and thin string or twine for finer work. Sailors used their leisure hours to develop ways of tying knots that were both decorative and highly functional.

Lanyards (see pg. 19), for example, were used to secure anything movable that had to be carried aloft and could be made fast round the neck, shoulder, wrist or attached to a belt, allowing the sailor to work with both hands and minimizing the danger of losing irreplaceable articles overboard. Lanyards could be knotted in many different ways, allowing the individual sailor to mark any personal articles as his own.

The inventiveness and creativity can also be seen in the way sailors combined different knots to make netting for fishing nets and hammocks, or to form something as complex as a ladder (see pg. 130) from a single piece of rope.

Flat knots (see pg. 115) were used to make matting, which was found everywhere on board – to prevent chafing and slipping, nailed to the deck at gangways and companionways, to the sides of smaller boats to act as buffers, and rails and spars. Vitally necessary and absolutely functional, mats were often as elegant in their patterns and formation as works of art.

Knotting on board ship was often very competitive and the secrets and intricacies of particular knots jealously guarded. Sailors were also responsible for the colourful descriptive names still given to particular knots, the Turk's Head (see pg. 89) and Monkey's Fist (see pg. 79), for example.

The Turk's Head, a tubular binding knot, combines a highly decorative appearance with a great diversity of practical uses. It is formed around a cylindrical object and was used as a foot hold on ladders, as a hand hold on life lines and guard rails, a hand grip on oars and fishing rods, a hand guard, drip guard and handle. The knot is so decorative, however, it was also commonly used, as it is today, in making bracelets, anklets, rings and napkin holders.

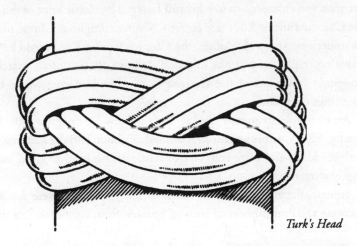

Turk's Head

The Monkey's Fist, the highly descriptive name refers to its shape, superficially resembles the Turk's Head but is formed around a small heavy ball and was used to carry the weight of a heaving line. It can be used to cover any small round objects, from paperweights to cane heads and door handles.

Sailors also spent their time in the plaiting or braiding of rope, which is termed Sinnet (see pg. 99). On board ship sinnet served many purposes; as lashing, as belting and to prevent chafing. It has excellent "cling" qualities and is resistant to surface wear. The intricacy that can be introduced into the plaiting or braiding process meant that sinnet work was often highly decorative.

By the middle of the nineteenth century, the great days of sail were coming to an end. Fast clipper ships and then the advent of steam meant sailors no longer had the time or the raw materials available for knot making. These changes did not mark the death of the craft, however, for sailors were not the only people interested in, or open to the functional and decorative possibilities of fancy knot work.

Their inland counterparts, working canals and rivers, made similar knots, adapted to their own style and purpose, as did other groups of workers with rope and time on their hands, from riggers to cow hands.

Decorative and fancy knotting had always been a part of the domestic arts and handicrafts. Knots were commonly used in dress making and the design of accessories, belts, bags, etc, even jewelry. The knots were not there just to decorate and enhance but to hold and fasten. The classic knot of this type was the Chinese Button Knot (see pg. 70). Worn throughout China, particularly on underwear and nightclothes, the Chinese Button Knot could be used as a fastening, replacing buttons of wood or bone. It was often matched with frogging – a variant of flat knotting – to provide decorative and unusual fastenings on coats.

Another knot frequently used in dress and jewelry design was the Bowknot (see pg. 52). Bowknots were often formed of ribbon and the material, together with the loops and loose ends characteristic of this kind of knot, made them highly attractive.

Sinnets, flat matting and all kinds of fancy knotting were freely used to decorate and embellish in all areas of fashion, from clothes to hair design.

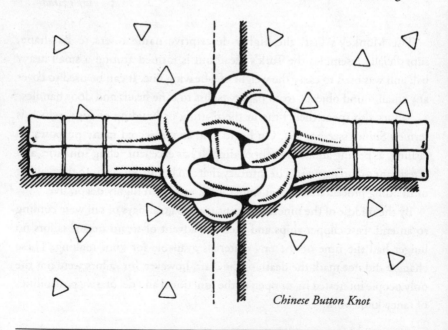

Chinese Button Knot

THE PRESENT DAY

D ecorative knots are as popular now as they were in the past. Modern sailors and boat owners rarely go to sea in fully rigged tall ships but they use the same knots as were used in the days when all craft were under sail. This is not just because of the proven reliability of knots developed in those times, but also because they recognise the knots' decorative potential. A knotted boat fender, for example, might do the same job but it looks significantly more attractive than an old tire. The Turk's Head, sinnets and lanyard knots all have their place on modern boats. Hammocks and rope ladders are just as important on board today as they were in the days of sail. Decorative knots are not only serviceable and functional but also enhance the ship-shape appearance of any vessel.

Knife Lanyard Knot

Outdoorsmen also find many uses for decorative knots. Lanyards are as useful halfway up a mountain as they are in the rigging of a ship, allowing free use of the hands while keeping vital belongings or equipment safe and secure. Knots, such as the Turk's Head again, or the Monkey's Fist, provide useful coverings and bindings, and sinnets and lanyard knots can be used to make belts and strong, attractive handles and strapping for gear.

Decorative knotting is not just found outdoors. It has become well established in arts and crafts generally and has a particularly strong place in interior design. Plant holders, curtain cords and tiebacks, cord pulls, light pulls, tassels and fringing, place mats on tables, even door mats and flooring are just some of the modern applications described in *The Book of Decorative Knots*. Many of the knots to be found in the book can be a help around the house generally, from wrapping gifts and parcels more attractively to getting the tail of a kite to fly right.

Similarly, decorative knots are still widely used in dress making, tailoring and the manufacture of personal accessories from belts and key fobs to hair ornaments. Knowing how to tie them, and when and where to apply them, allows the individual scope for ingenuity and creativity in making gifts and personal items and can, in fact, become a whole hobby area in its own right.

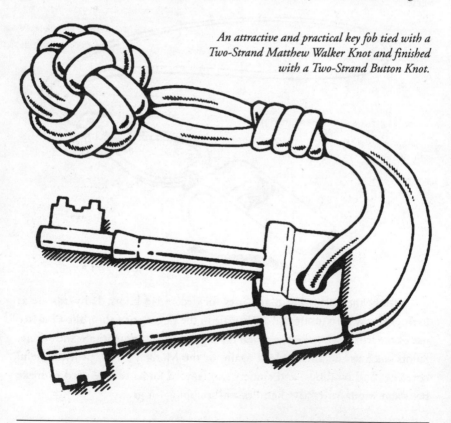

An attractive and practical key fob tied with a Two-Strand Matthew Walker Knot and finished with a Two-Strand Button Knot.

MATERIALS

It is possible to make decorative knots out of almost anything from rope and leather to human hair, but the most common materials are rope of different thicknesses, along with yarn, braid, string, cord, thread and twine (known as small stuff). Decorative knotting also utilizes materials not generally associated with ordinary knot formation, such as flat tape and ribbon.

NATURAL FIBER ROPES

Traditionally, rope was made from vegetable fibers and on the old sailing ships this was what would be used for decorative knotting. Sailors would use whatever material was at hand, the most commonly available being manila, sisal, coir and hemp. Flax and cotton were highly prized for their fine quality and manageability, but they were expensive and more likely to be used to rig a rich man's yacht than on an ordinary sailing vessel.

Three-strand natural fiber rope.

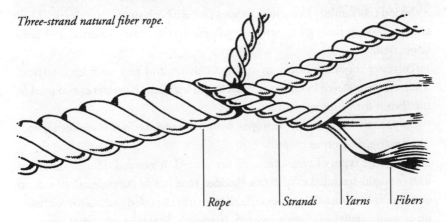

| *Rope* | *Strands* | *Yarns* | *Fibers* |

Natural fiber rope is normally three-strand and right laid and is made by twisting fibers of natural materials together. The fibers were twisted first into yarn, then into strands, and finally into rope, in a process called laying up. Sailors often had to use spoiled or junk rope which could be any size for their own knot tying and would carefully unravel the laid up rope and then work it up themselves into the size they required.

Nowadays, natural rope is little used for conventional knots, but for decorative purposes many still prefer vegetable fibers for their traditional appearance and beauty of their natural colors and textures. The finest natural fibers are cotton, linen and silk.

SYNTHETIC ROPES

Synthetic materials have widely replaced natural fibers in the manufacture of rope. Man-made filaments can be spun to run the whole length of a line, do not vary in thickness, and do not have to be twisted together to make them cohere. This gives them superior strength.

Nylon, developed toward the end of the Second World War, was the first man-made material to be used in this way. Since then a range of synthetic ropes have been developed to meet different purposes, but they all share certain characteristics. Size for size they are lighter, stronger and cheaper than their natural counterparts. They can also be made in a range of colors, and this makes them particularly attractive for the tying of decorative knots.

Nylon (Polyamide) fibers make ropes that are both strong and elastic. They are also used in fishing line, and are tough, flexible, easily knotted and hold knots well.

Polyester ropes are nearly as strong as nylon and give very little stretch. They are widely used in sailing for sheets and halyards. Polyester is also used in small stuff for whipping twine.

Polypropylene is not as strong as nylon or polyester but it makes a good, inexpensive, all-purpose rope.

The other types of synthetic rope are plaited or braided. Plaited describes four- or eight-stranded solid plaits. Braided rope has an outer sheath of sixteen or more strands round an inner core that is either braided and hollow or made up of solid parallel, or slightly twisted, filaments. Braided rope is the softer and more flexible of the two types of rope.

Both natural fiber and synthetic ropes are suited to and used for different types of decorative knotting. Natural fiber ropes are usually only available from ship and boat chandlers or specialist rope suppliers. Synthetic ropes are more widely available, from camping and climbing shops to D.I.Y stores.

SMALL STUFF

Small stuff, the name given to any rope under an inch (25mm) in circumference, is used for fine work. It includes cord, string, thread, twine and yarn. Again it can be either man-made or natural fiber and is available from craft shops, camping shops, hardware stores, fishing tackle shops. Thread and yarn can also be bought in haberdashers, knitting and dressmaking shops.

RIBBON AND TAPE

Ribbon and different widths of tape are also used in decorative and fancy knot work and are available in a wide variety of colors. They would normally be bought in dressmaking, knitting and craft shops.

CHOOSING MATERIALS

The choice of materials very much depends on the type of knot you want to tie, what it will be used for, and the effect you wish to create. The same knot can look startlingly different, depending on the material used. Ribbon, for example, works up very differently from rope.

A Bowknot tied with ribbon.

A Bowknot tied with cord.

SEALING ENDS

Sealing the ends, if necessary, of your tying material makes knots significantly easier to tie as well as giving a neater appearance. When you buy synthetic rope from a chandlers, they will cut it to the length you require with an electrically heated knife. This seals the ends and gives a sharp edge. When you cut synthetic rope yourself, use a sharp knife and then melt the end with a cigarette lighter or on an electric ring.

Natural fiber rope will fray if left unseized. A neat, secure and easy way to prevent this is by whipping the ends. Use vegetable fiber twine and always bind against the lay of the rope. In general whipping needs to be as long as the width of the rope.

Two other quick and efficient methods of sealing ends is to use ordinary adhesive tape or on small stuff, a simple stopper knot.

Whipping the end of a rope.

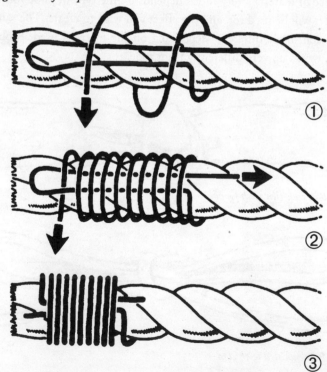

SELECTING KNOTS

Knots are selected according to function, purpose and decorative effect. *The Book of Decorative Knots* illustrates 50 of the best known and commonly tied knots, clearly explains how to tie them and describes their uses, functions and applications. No amount of theoretical knowledge, however, can compensate for practical experience. Mastering anything takes practice and tying knots is no exception. A beginner should not be discouraged if he or she is not immediately successful with a complicated knot, but it does make sense to master the simpler versions of each knot first.

A loosely tied Chinese Button Knot (left) *and the final 'worked' version* (right).

Finally, never try to complete an elaborate knot in one operation or draw it up in one movement. A knot should be loosely tied or projected and then "worked", molded carefully to keep its shape as it is gradually drawn up to final tightness. Slack should be worked out evenly and gradually. In decorative knotting this is as important as correct tying and requires both patience and practice.

HOW TO USE THIS BOOK

The diagrams accompanying the descriptions of the knots are intended to be self-explanatory. Written instructions, special tying techniques and methods will accompany the more complex knots. There are arrows to show the directions in which you should push or pull the working ends of the rope or line. The dotted lines indicate intermediate positions of the rope. Always follow the order shown of going over or under a length of line; reversing or changing this order could result in a completely different knot.

ROPE PARTS

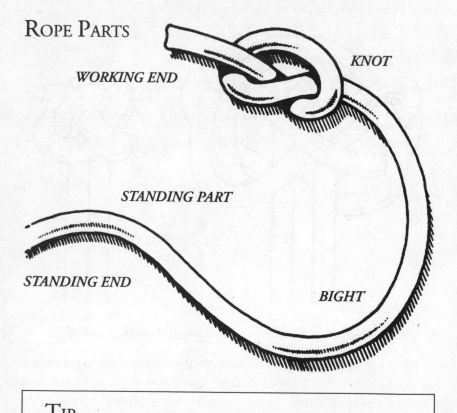

WORKING END

KNOT

STANDING PART

STANDING END

BIGHT

TIP . . . .

Metal or plastic tipped round shoelaces are excellent for knot practice. They are obtainable in a range of colors and different lengths.

1
LANYARD KNOTS

A lanyard is usually worn around the neck or attached to a belt for the purpose of holding a wide variety of objects – from knives and whistles to watches and binoculars. Because the cord is left in view it is often decorated with a range of elaborate lanyard knots and sinnets (see pg. 99).

The lanyard knots illustrated in this chapter divide into two groups, single-strand and two-strand.

Double Knife Lanyard Knot

MULTIPLE OVERHAND KNOT

This knot, also known as the blood knot, can be tied with any number of turns. A small knot, as shown here with four turns, can be gently drawn together by keeping the knot open and loose and pulling on both ends at the same time – it also helps to form the knot by twisting the two ends in opposite directions as you pull. Larger knots with more turns must be slowly "worked" together in order for the knot to settle into its final form.

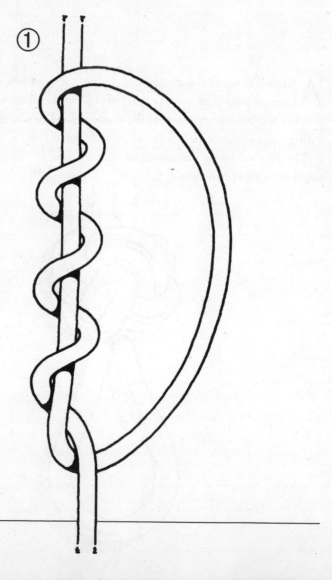

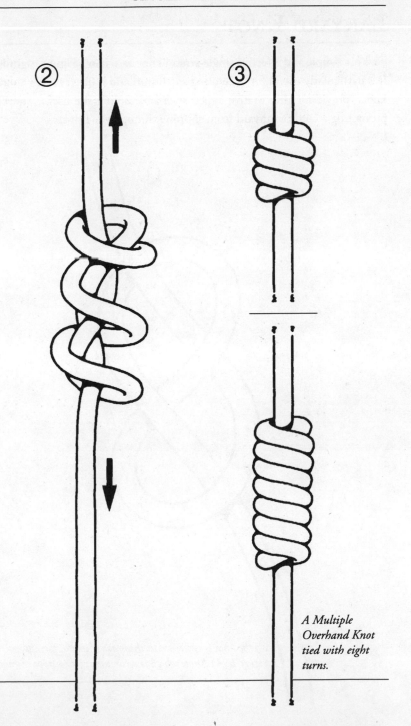

*A Multiple
Overhand Knot
tied with eight
turns.*

LANYARD KNOT

This is a simple and effective single-strand knot based on a Figure-Eight Knot. It is particularly useful for decorating small stuff and is often tied in a series of knots, providing a decorative appearance and serving the useful purpose of preventing a cord or lanyard from slipping through the fingers.

If the knot is tightened at this stage it would form a Figure-Eight Knot, which is a commonly used stopper knot.

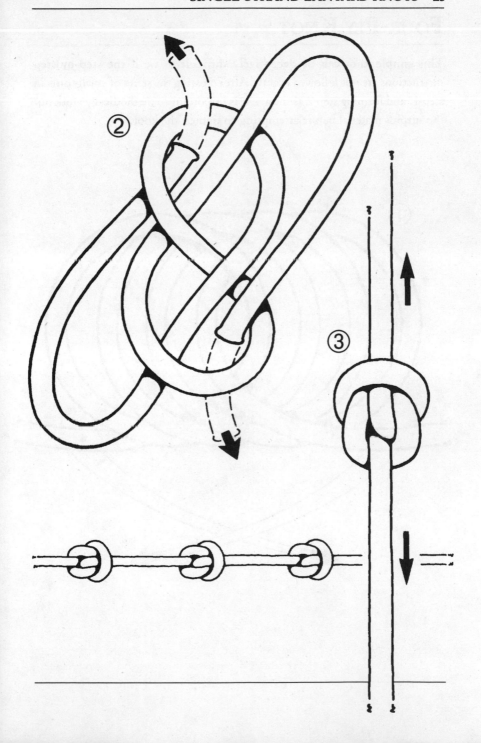

FOUR-PLY KNOT

This simple knot can be deceptively difficult to tie if the step-by-step instructions are not followed exactly. After creating the series of small turns in step 1, and forming step 2 as shown, it is important to methodically work out the surplus material before attempting to tighten the knot.

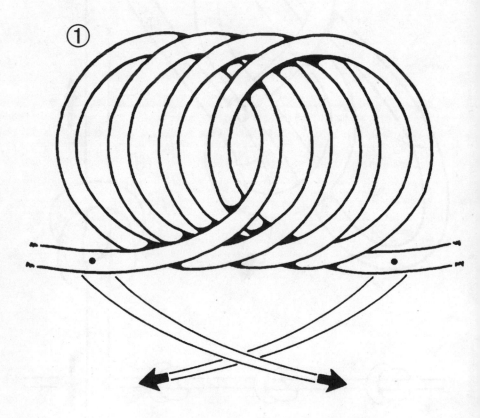

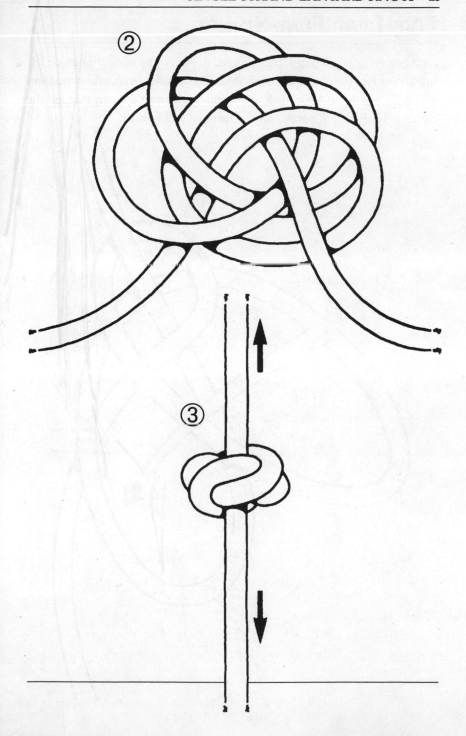

FIVE-LEAD FLAT-SINNET

Arrange the cord as in step 1, then proceed to plait by twisting the outside left strand over into the center. Then twist the new outside left strand over to form step 2. To finish the knot, tuck the outside right strand down through the center, gradually work out the surplus material and tighten.

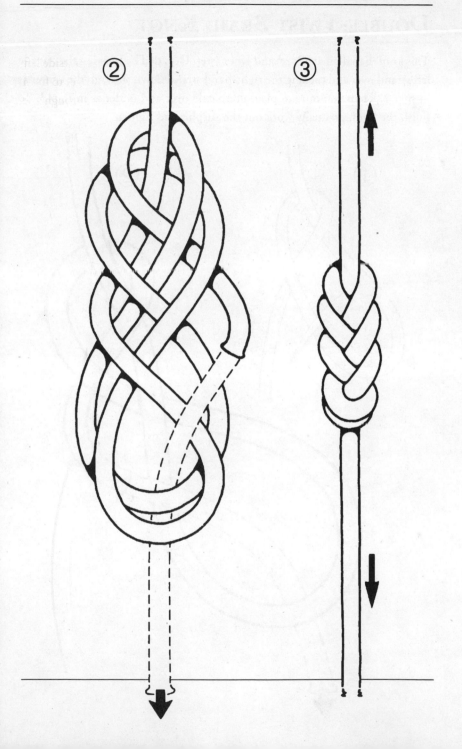

DOUBLE-TWIST BRAID KNOT

This knot, based on an Overhand Knot (step 1), is tied by twisting the outside left strand over and tucking the right-hand strand down through the center as in step 2. Then continue to plait alternately over and under as in step 3. To finish the knot, gradually work out the surplus and tighten.

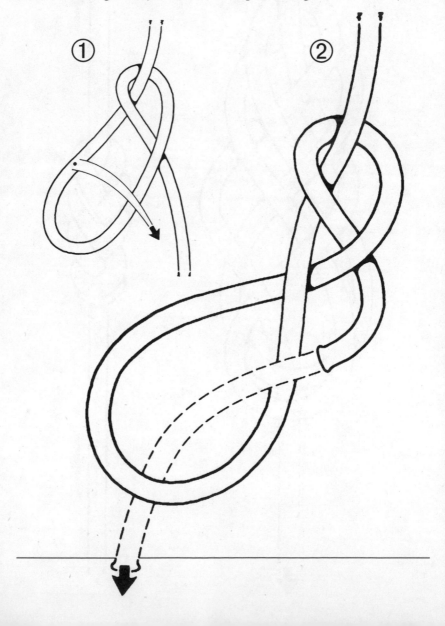

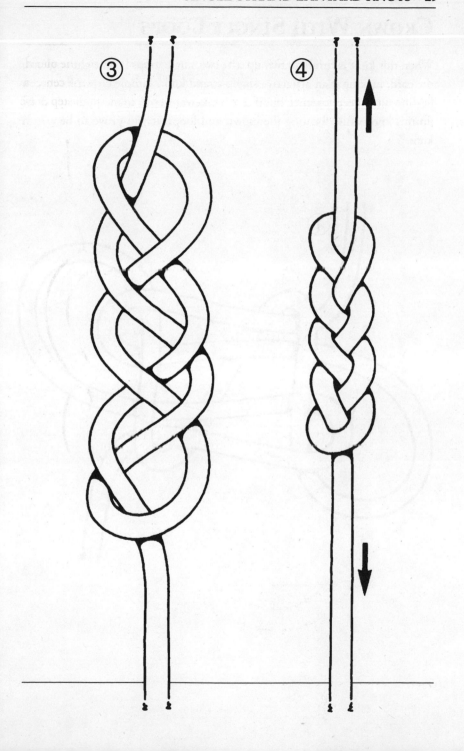

CROWN WITH SINGLE LOOPS

When this knot is firmly drawn up, the two single loops lie at right angles to the cord, making it an attractive single-strand knot. Simple crown knots can be difficult to keep together, but if care is taken at step 2, to methodically draw up this knot while forming the crown and loops, it will prove to be a firm knot.

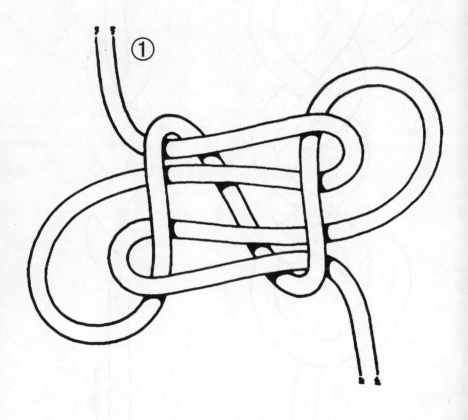

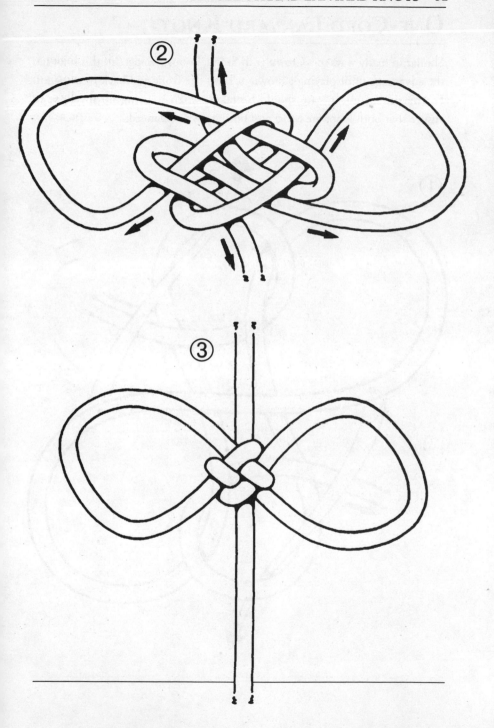

ONE-CORD LANYARD KNOT

Similar in many ways to a Crown with Single Loops (see pg. 30) this knot has the advantage of displaying a crown at both the front and back of the knot. For maximum effect, care should be taken when drawing up the knot to ensure that both loops are equal and both crowns balanced.

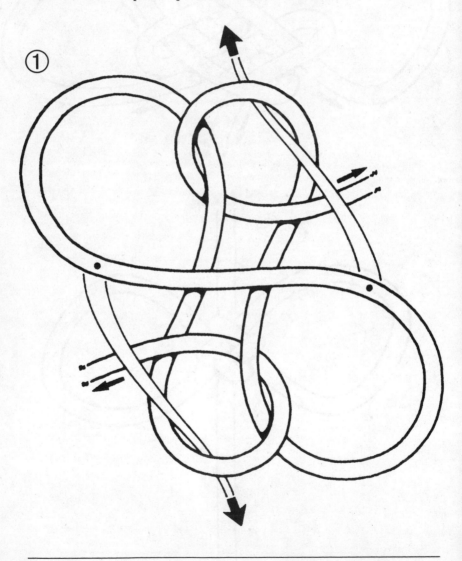

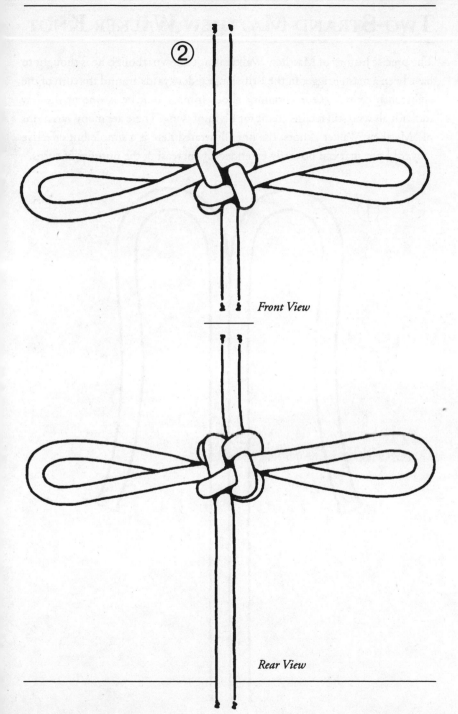

Front View

Rear View

TWO-STRAND MATTHEW WALKER KNOT

The precise history of Matthew Walker is not known, though he is thought to have been a master rigger in the British naval dockyards around the turn of the eighteenth century. One certainty about him, is that he is one of the few individuals who still retains credit for his knot tying. There are many variations of "Matthew Walker" knots; the one illustrated here is a simple but effective lanyard knot that can be easily extended by increasing the number of turns.

①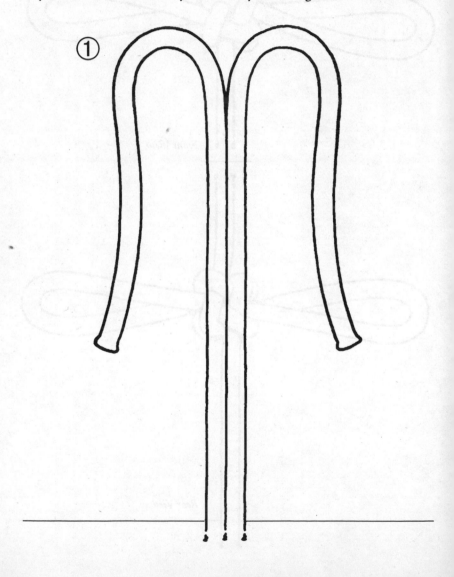

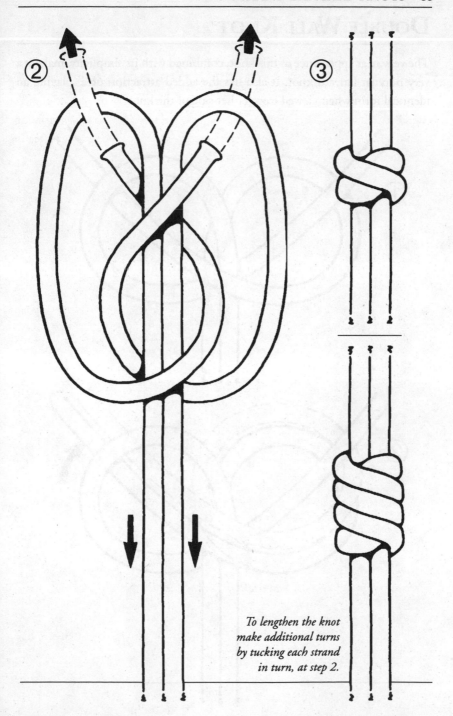

*To lengthen the knot
make additional turns
by tucking each strand
in turn, at step 2.*

DOUBLE WALL KNOT

The very neat appearance of this knot, combined with its simplicity, make it a very popular lanyard knot. It also has the added attraction of displaying an identical form when viewed from either side of the knot.

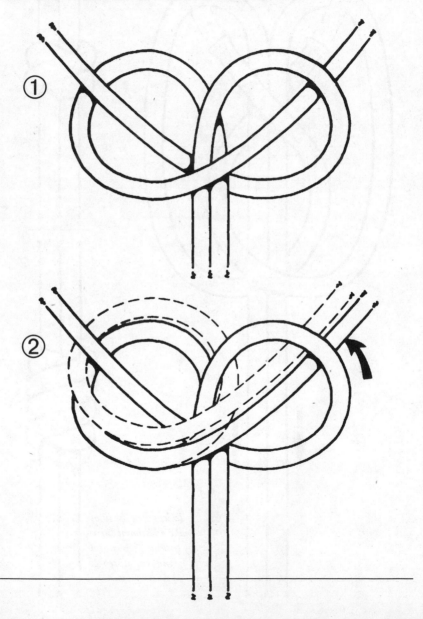

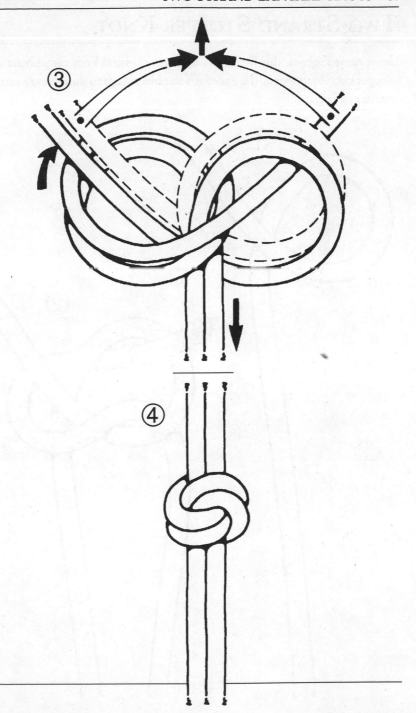

TWO-STRAND STOPPER KNOT

As its name suggests, this flat, wide, decorative lanyard knot can also act as a stopper knot. Stopper knots are useful if an object needs to slide along a certain length of a lanyard.

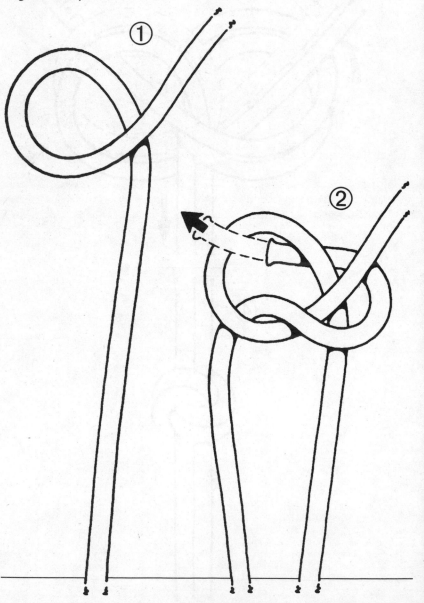

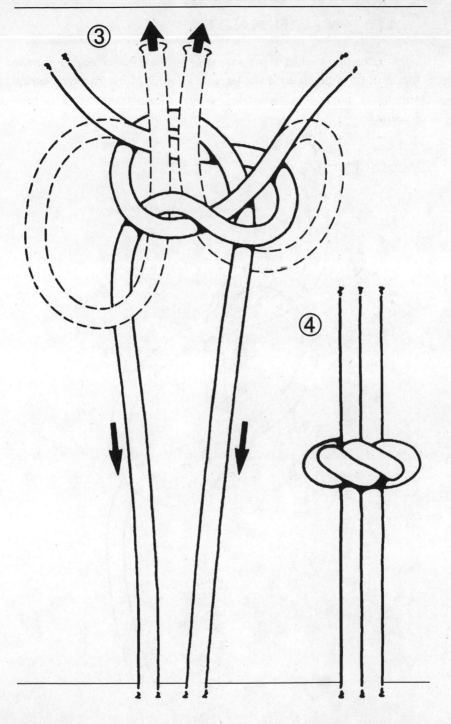

FLAT LANYARD KNOT

This attractive knot, which is based on two Overhand Knots, enables the two lanyard cords to be parted. In order to achieve the distinctive symmetrical form, the knot must be methodically "worked" together, after step 2 has been completed.

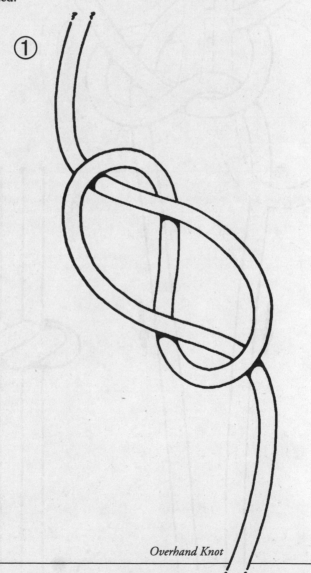

①

Overhand Knot

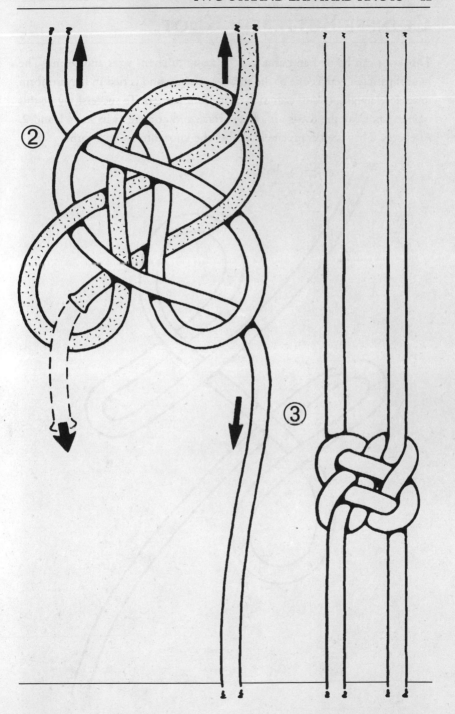

② ③

CHINESE BUTTERFLY KNOT

This knot can be tied and arranged in many different sizes and forms. The knot illustrated here is one of the smaller versions and is tied in lanyard form to achieve a bight, or curve, at each of the four corners. To successfully tie this type of knot, lay the cords on a flat surface and arrange as in steps 1 and 2. After step 2 has been completed, "work" the knot into its final form.

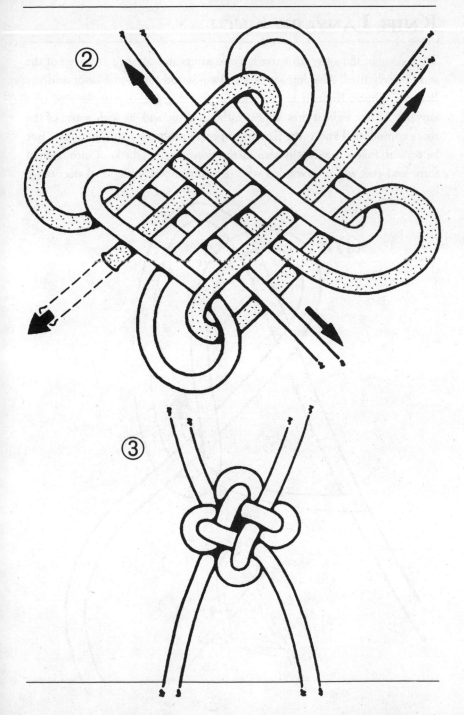

KNIFE LANYARD KNOT

This is one of the most attractive lanyard knots and subsequently one of the most widely used. Also known as the Two-Strand Diamond Knot and the Bosun's Whistle Knot, it is excellent for forming the loop at the end of a lanyard. At first sight it may appear difficult to tie and, as with many of the more complicated knots, the first attempt will probably result in failure. But be patient, follow the step-by-step instructions, "work" the knot into its final form and you will be rewarded with a beautiful and functional decorative knot.

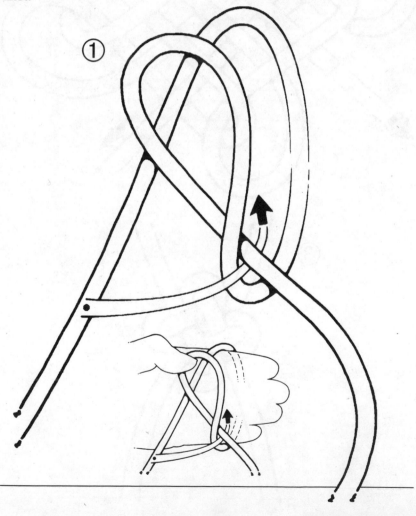

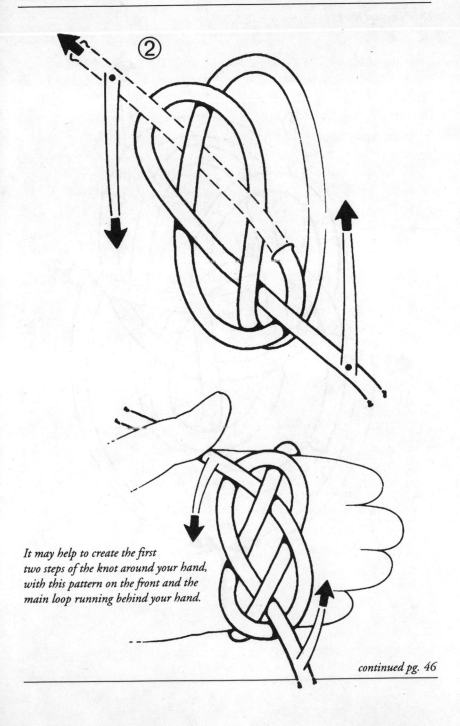

It may help to create the first
two steps of the knot around your hand,
with this pattern on the front and the
main loop running behind your hand.

continued pg. 46

Knife Lanyard Knot

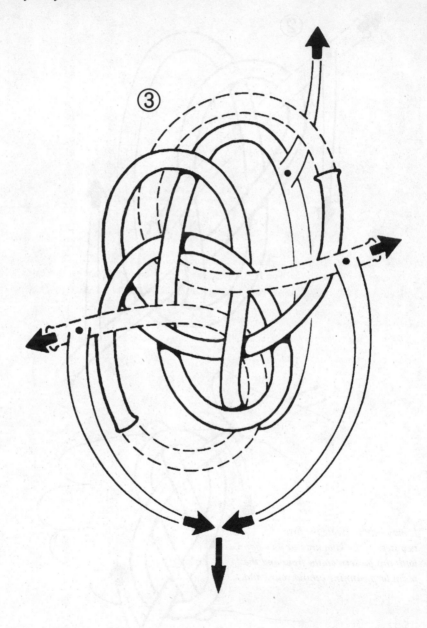

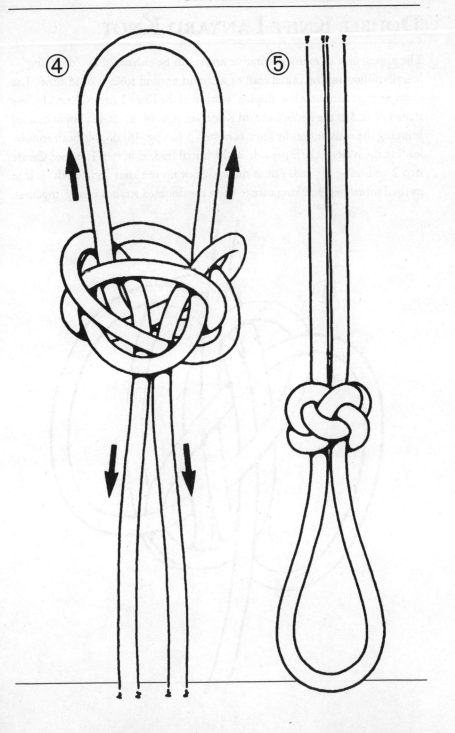

④

⑤

DOUBLE KNIFE LANYARD KNOT

The appearance of many decorative knots can be enhanced by "doubling" – literally following the initial lead of a strand around for a second time. The example illustrated here is a "double" version of the Knife Lanyard Knot. Follow steps 1, 2 & 3 of the Knife Lanyard Knot (see pgs. 44, 45 & 46) but instead of bringing the ends out of the knot as in step 3 (see pg. 46) double both ends by leading them along the inner side of the initial lead, as in step 1, below. Create step 2 and bring the ends out as shown, draw up the knot and "work" it into its final form, step 3, taking care to keep the doubled strands neatly together.

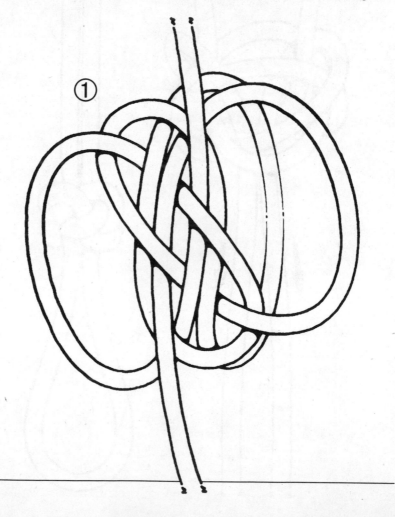

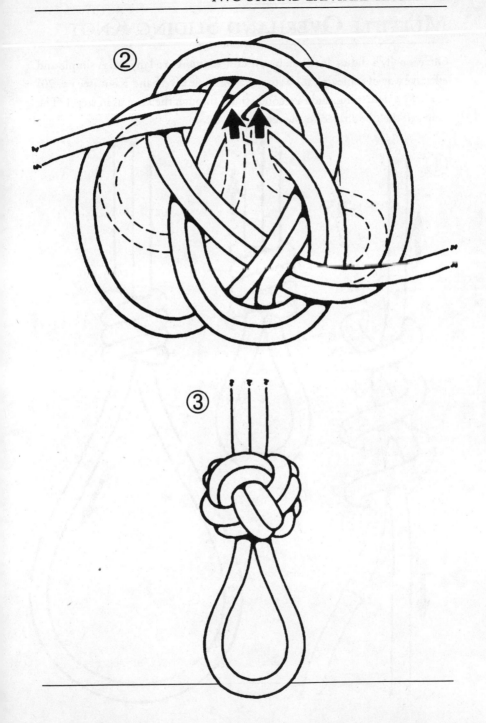

MULTIPLE OVERHAND SLIDING KNOT

Occasionally a sliding loop can be a useful addition to a lanyard. A simple and effective way of achieving this is to use a Multiple Overhand Knot (see pg. 20) but before tightening, slide a second strand through the knot as in step 1. The loop can then be altered to the required size.

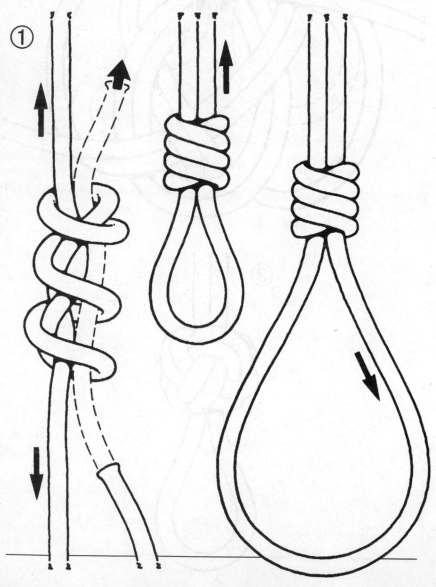

2

BOWKNOTS

T he common characteristics of Bowknots, often called "Fancy" knots, are the harmonious and symmetrical forms that are created from bows, loops and crowns. They are regularly used to give that "final touch" when wrapping gifts or parcels. The following examples can be tied in a wide variety of materials, keeping in mind that if ribbon or a patterned material having one definite right side is used, it will be necessary to twist the material and arrange the knot to keep that side uppermost.

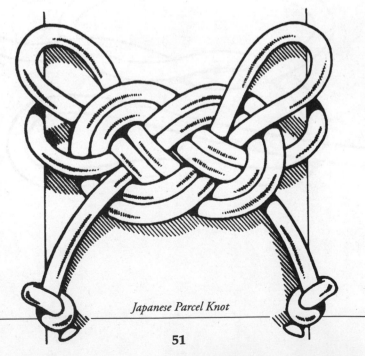

Japanese Parcel Knot

BOWKNOT

The common or ordinary bowknot is one of the most widely used of all knots. It can be used in any situation that requires two working ends to be quickly and easily tied together, plus it has the added advantage of being equally as easy to untie, by simply pulling on one of the working ends.

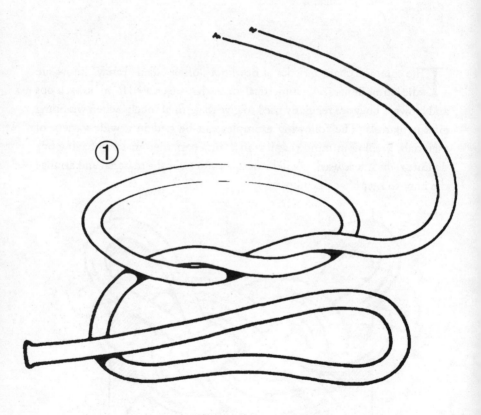

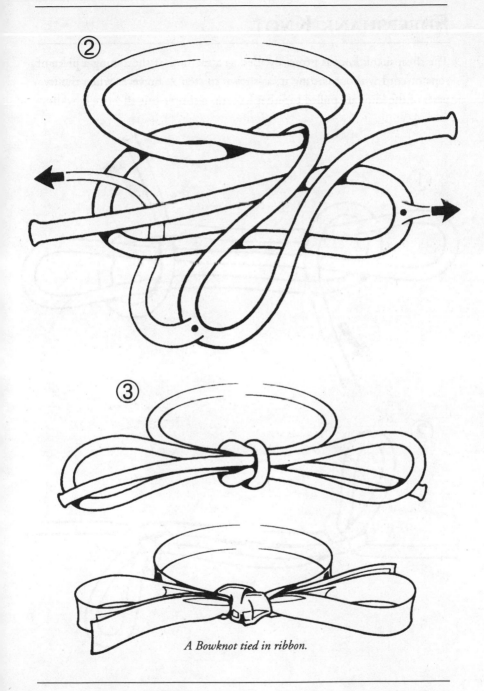

A Bowknot tied in ribbon.

SHEEPSHANK KNOT

The sheepshank knot is primarily used as a method of shortening a piece of rope or cord without cutting it, as shown in step 2, however when the two parts of the knot are pulled together it forms a simple but effective bowknot.

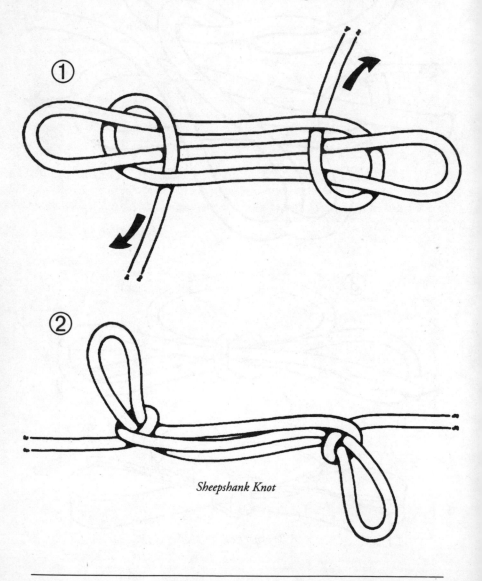

Sheepshank Knot

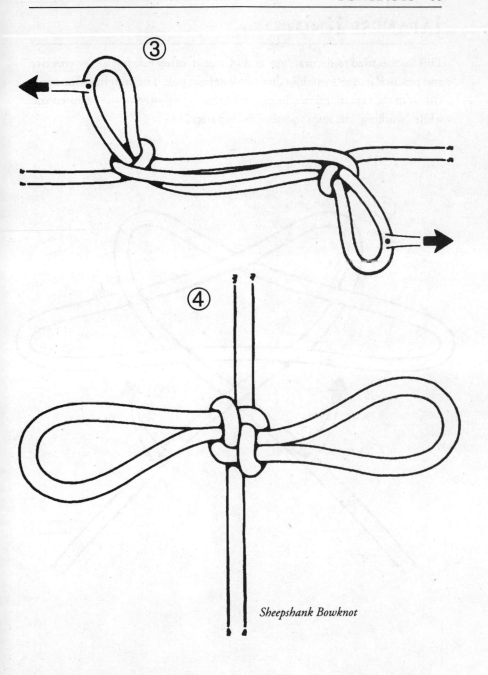

Sheepshank Bowknot

JAPANESE KNOT

This knot is used to decorate the end of a cord, often making a very effective and practical end to a window shade pull or light pull. The knot has a four-part crown in the center and two loops which can be adjusted to the required size while "working" the knot together during step 2.

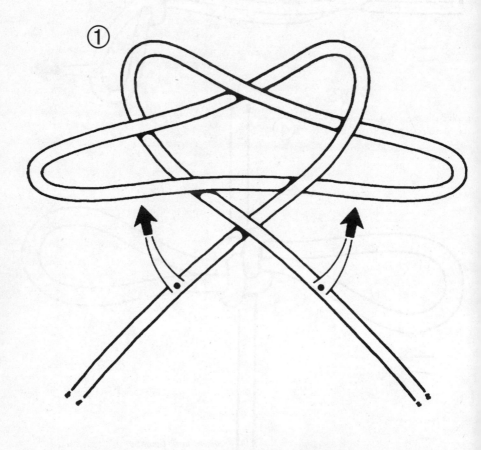

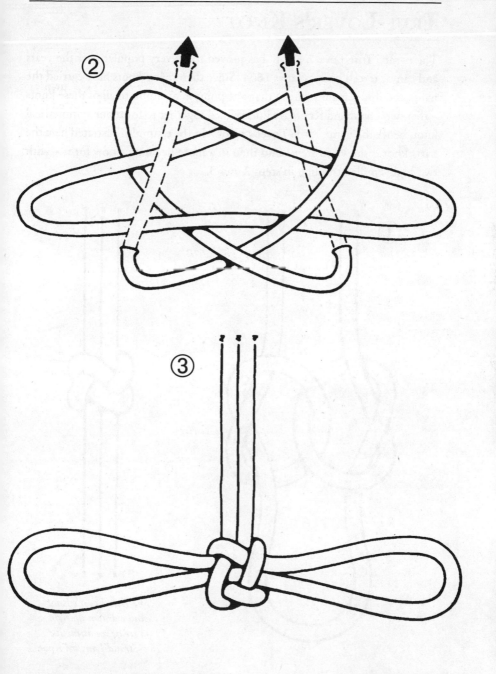

TRUE-LOVER'S KNOT

The name "True-Lover's Knot" has proved to be very popular over the years and can be traced back as far as 1664. Since then many knots have carried the name and it is generally agreed that one point is common to all of these knots – that two Overhand Knots are intertwined together to form one symmetrical knot, hence the name "True-Lover's Knot." In the example illustrated here the basic knot is shown in step 1 and then in a more decorative bow form – with two bights pulled through in steps 2 and 3.

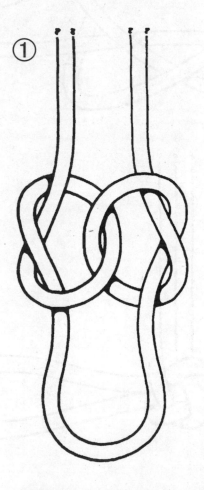

①

The True-Lover's Knot can be drawn up tight to create an attractive Two-Strand Lanyard Knot.

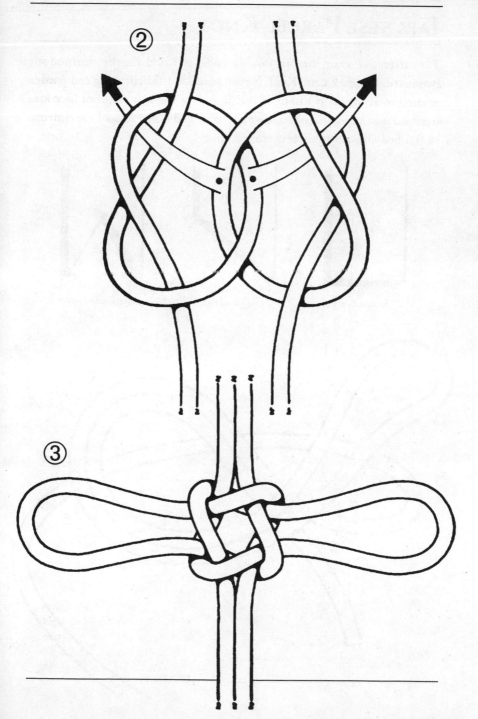

JAPANESE PARCEL KNOT

This attractive knot, tied in double ends, is based on the distinctively symmetrical Carrick Bend Knot. It is an ideal knot for gift tying and is often referred to as the "Gift Knot." If tied in ribbon the two ends can be cut or trimmed into a diagonal or swallowtail shape, and if tied in cord the ends can be finished off with a simple overhand knot.

Uncut ribbon   *Diagonal cut*   *Swallowtail cut*

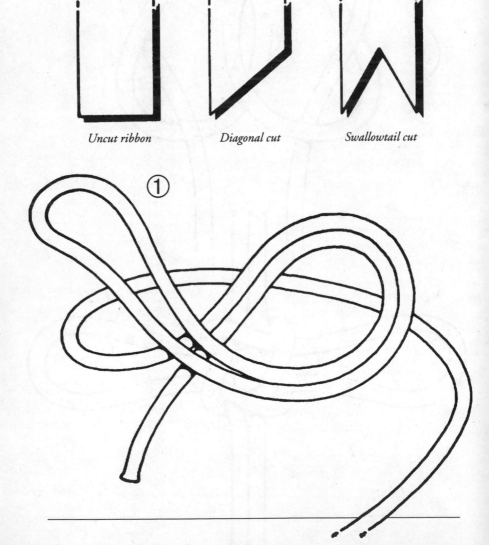

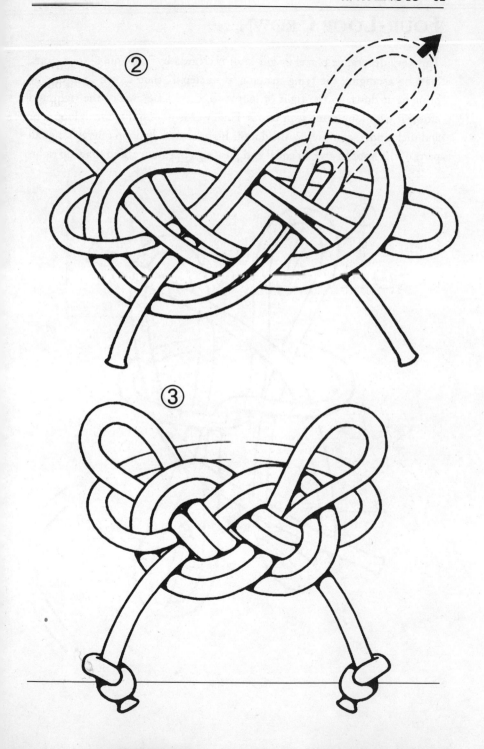

FOUR-LOOP CROWN

This very decorative parcel or gift knot is created by "crowning" four loops. Start by arranging the tying material as in step 1, then crown loop one by bringing it down to the right of loop two, cross loop two to the right and crown it with loop three as in step 2. Finally crown loop three with loop four and tuck under, as in step 2, the double bight created by loop one. Arrange all parts of the knot to give an equal and pleasing appearance, and draw up tight.

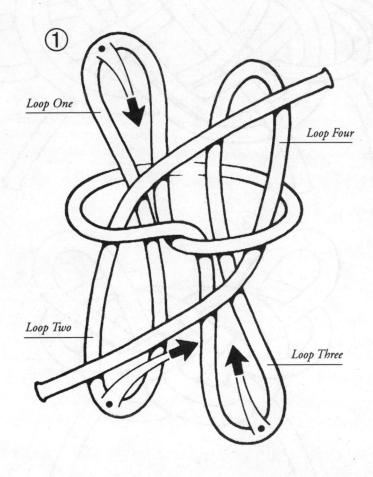

Loop One

Loop Four

Loop Two

Loop Three

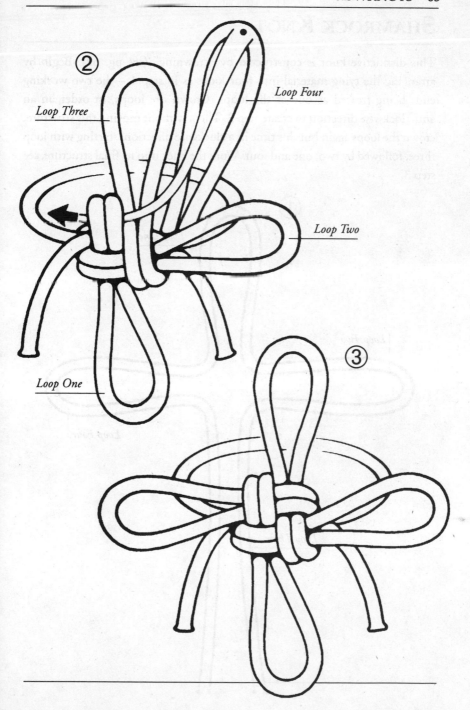

② *Loop Three* *Loop Four* *Loop Two* *Loop One*

③

Shamrock Knot

This distinctive knot is constructed by "crowning" (see pg. 62). Begin by arranging the tying material into four loops as in step 1 – the two working ends being treated as one of the loops. Crown the loops, in order, in an anti-clockwise direction to create step 2. Then, without moving this structure, crown the loops again but this time in a clockwise direction, starting with loop three, followed by two, one and four. Work the knot into its final structure, see step 3.

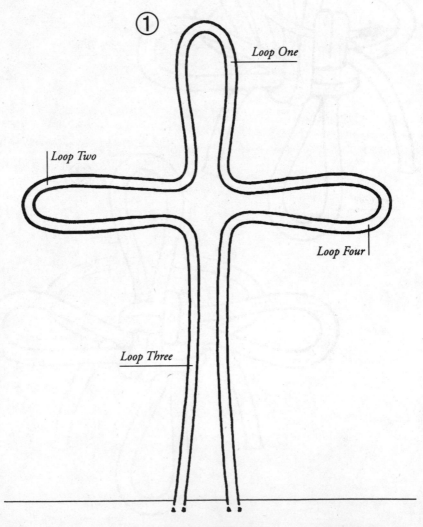

① Loop One

Loop Two

Loop Four

Loop Three

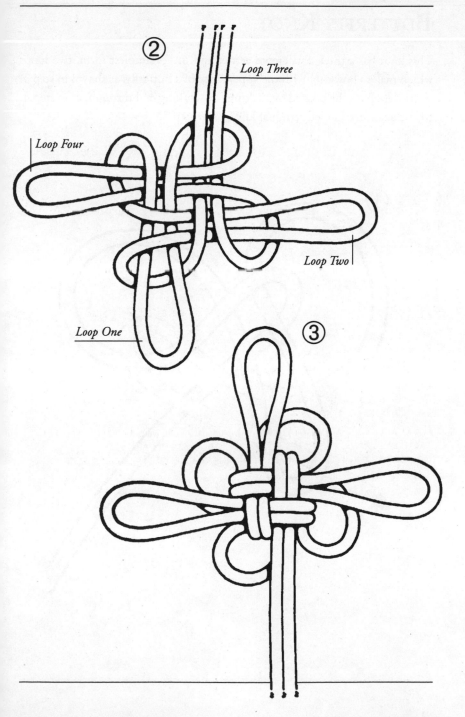

② Loop Three

Loop Four

Loop Two

Loop One

③

BUTTERFLY KNOT

This knot has a three-part crown center and, in its simplest form, two loops which make a bowknot with the appearance of a butterfly, as shown in step 3. A third loop can be created by tucking the working end through, as in step 4, to create a three looped terminal knot, as in step 5.

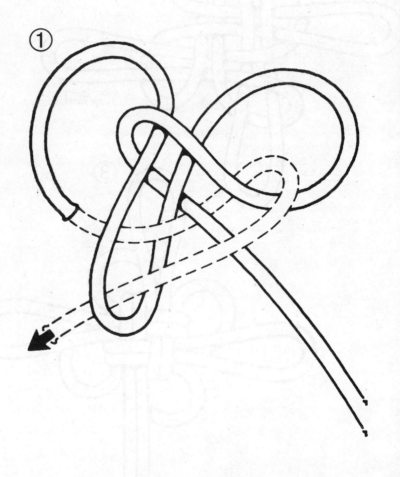

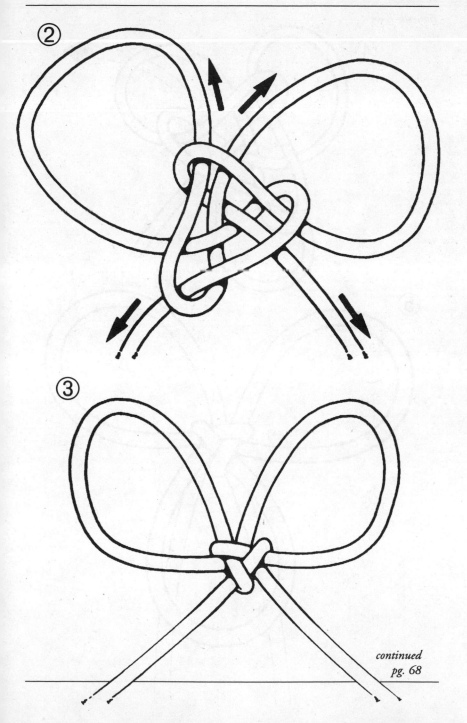

②

③

continued
pg. 68

Butterfly Knot

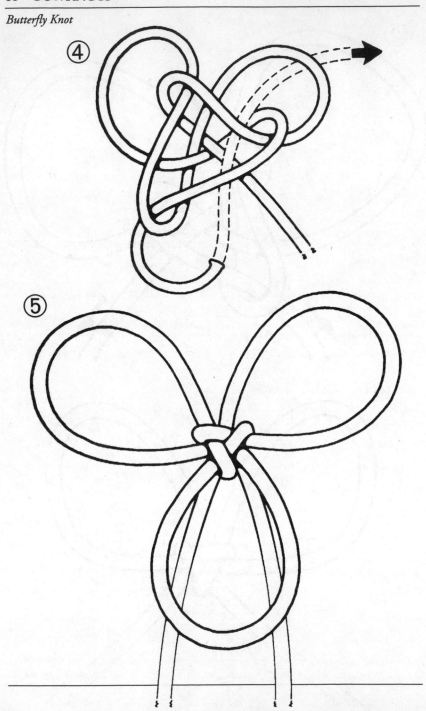

3

BUTTON KNOTS

. . . .

B utton knots, or Pajama knots, are exactly as their name suggests – round, symmetrical knots used to form buttons to hold or fasten garments together, in particular, underwear and night clothes. Buttons of this type are still worn throughout China and are often seen as fashionable accessories elsewhere in the world. As well as being highly decorative, these buttons are softer and more comfortable to wear than bone or plastic buttons and have the advantage of being virtually unbreakable.

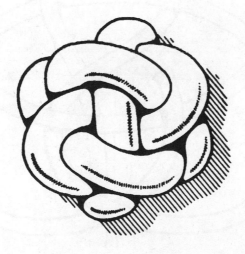

Chinese Button Knot

CHINESE BUTTON KNOT

Tying the traditional Chinese Button Knot as shown here may require a few attempts before the necessary technique is achieved. Start by creating step 1 on a flat surface. Then let the two ends drop down to form a stem as in step 2. Slowly work out the surplus material, at first keeping the knot flat, then as the knot draws up, allow it to form a mushroom shape as in step 3. The mushroom shape is formed by the rim of the knot closing down and the center of the knot rising up. Work the knot into its final form, step 4, by drawing the knot up tightly. This is best achieved by using a pair of thin nosed pliers or, if the tying material is small and delicate, a pair of fine tweezers.

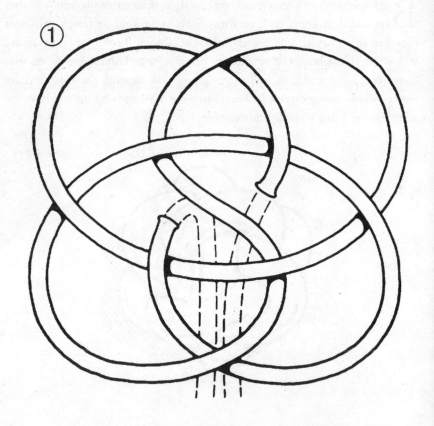

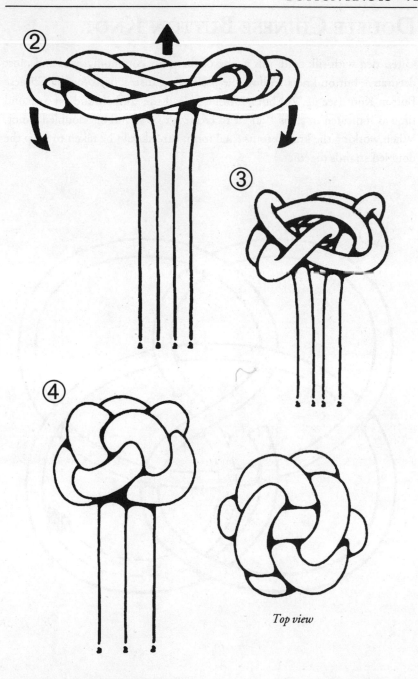

Top view

DOUBLE CHINESE BUTTON KNOT

Often tied with silk cord, this is one of the most commonly used and most decorative button knots. Follow the basic tying instructions for the Chinese Button Knot (see pg. 70) but continue to lead the cord around for a second time as indicated in steps 1 and 2 to create a two strand or "doubled" knot. When working the knot into its final form, care should be taken to keep the doubled strands together.

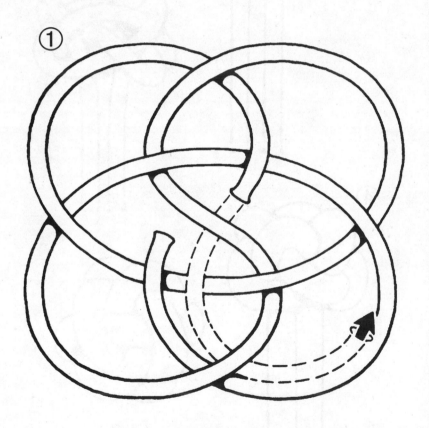

Top view

EIGHT-PART BUTTON KNOT

This knot is an interesting variation of the Chinese Button Knot and is created by changing the final tuck of the ends in step 1 – the rest of the tying instructions are as shown on page 70. The traditional Chinese Button Knot has nine surface parts, this knot has eight, altering the appearance enough to make it an alternative worth considering. Like the traditional knot, this one can also be "doubled."

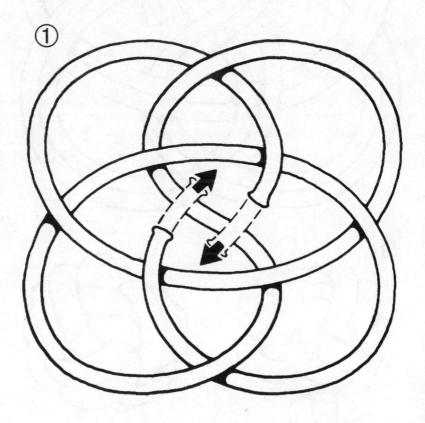

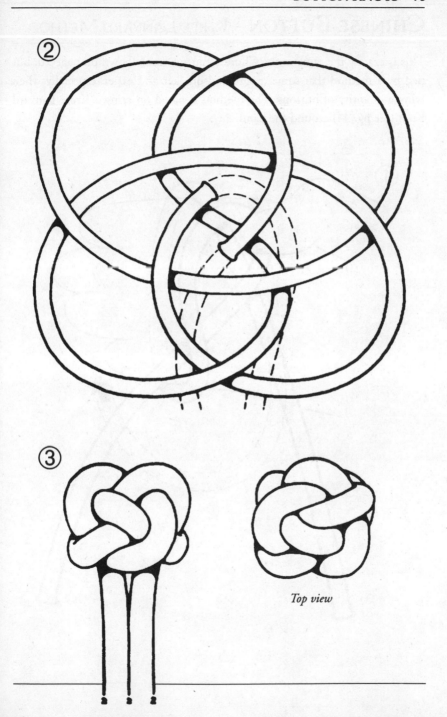

Top view

CHINESE BUTTON - KNIFE LANYARD METHOD

This is exactly the same as the Chinese Button Knot shown on page 70, but tied by a method that some might find quicker and easier, especially when tying a quantity of buttons. The method is based on tying a Knife Lanyard Knot (see pg. 44) around the hand.

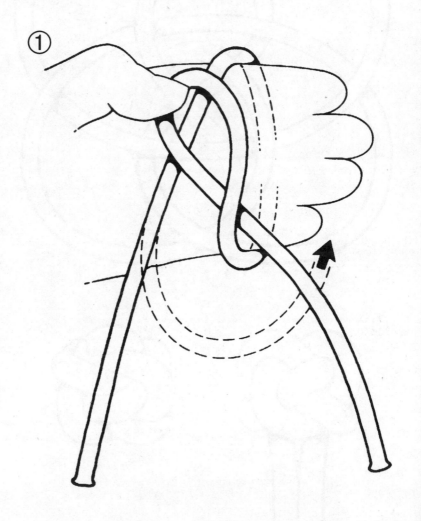

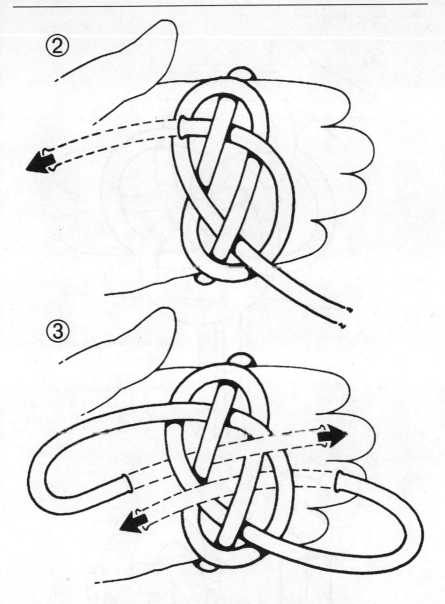

When the two ends have been pushed through, remove
the knot from the hand, turn it completely over, and place
the two ends between the two middle fingers as shown in step 4.

continued pg. 78

Chinese Button - Knife Lanyard Method

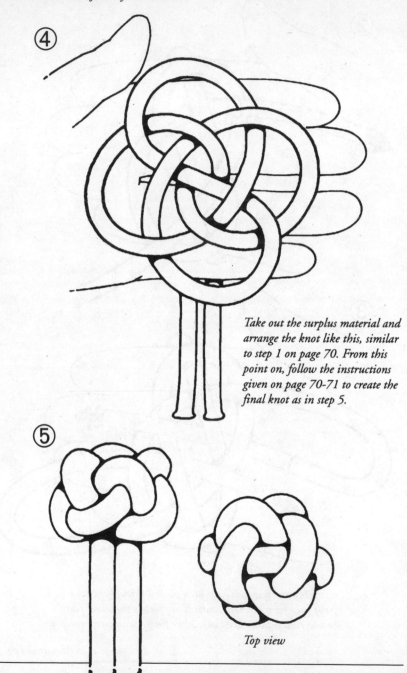

④

Take out the surplus material and arrange the knot like this, similar to step 1 on page 70. From this point on, follow the instructions given on page 70-71 to create the final knot as in step 5.

⑤

Top view

4
MONKEY'S FIST KNOTS

. . . .

The Monkey's Fist is a decorative knot that also has many practical uses, the most common being as the knot used at the end of a "heaving line," the line that is thrown from boat to shore or to another vessel. The purpose of the heaving line is to draw behind it a heavier line or rope to use for tying up. To give the Monkey's Fist more weight it is often tied over a spherical object such as a heavy ball or a stone, smaller knots can be tied over golf balls or marbles. Decoratively, it makes an attractive end to any cord, and is regularly used at the end of pull cords.

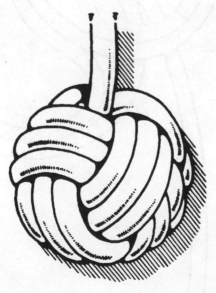

Monkey's Fist

MONKEY'S FIST - METHOD ONE

When using the traditional method of tying the Monkey's Fist, the knot is tied in two or three-ply. The illustrations here show a two-ply knot, but the tying instructions for three-ply are exactly the same. If required, a weight or core can be inserted at step 3. The knot needs to be carefully and methodically worked into its final symmetrical form, and if only one strand is required from the knot, the other strand can be worked around and tucked inside the knot to hide it.

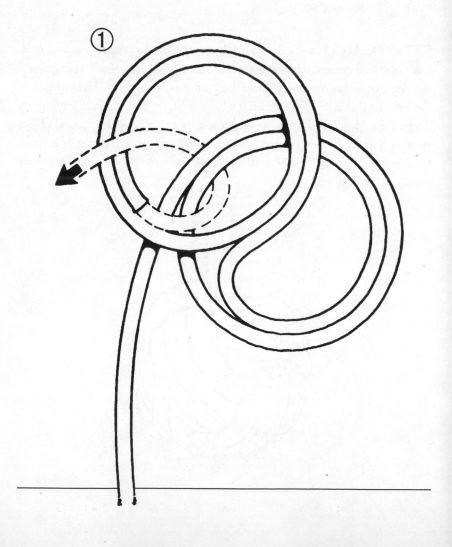

continued pg. 82

Monkey's Fist - Method One

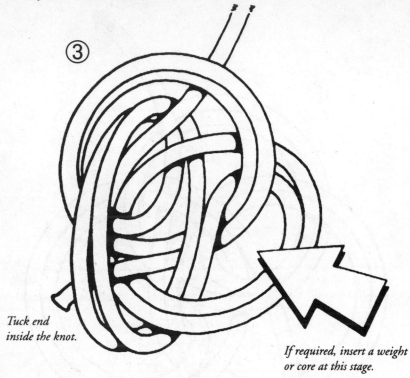

③

*Tuck end
inside the knot.*

*If required, insert a weight
or core at this stage.*

④

MONKEY'S FIST - METHOD TWO

This alternate way of tying a Monkey's Fist is shown in three-ply and with both ends being brought out of the knot. As with the first method, this knot can be tied around a weight or core object.

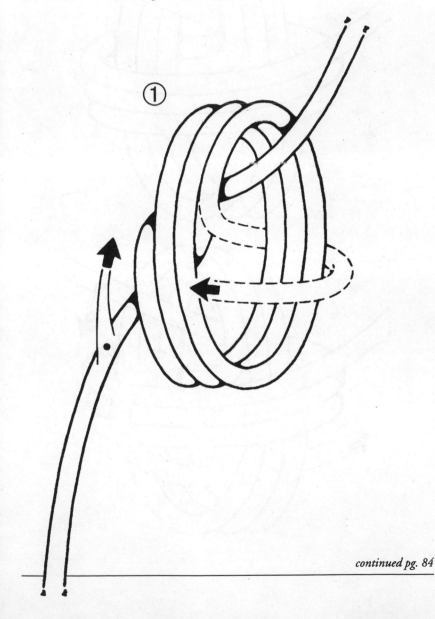

continued pg. 84

Monkey's Fist - Method Two

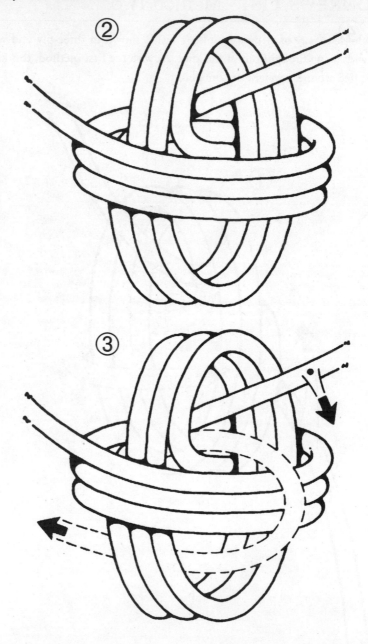

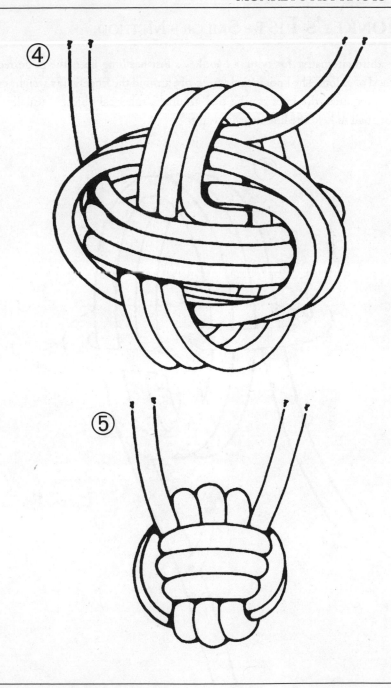

MONKEY'S FIST - SAILOR'S METHOD

This third alternative for tying a Monkey's Fist has long been the preferred method of sailors. The knot is tied, three-ply, around the fingers. If a weight or core is required, the knot can be tied around a spherical object – usually a rubber ball to help the line float in water.

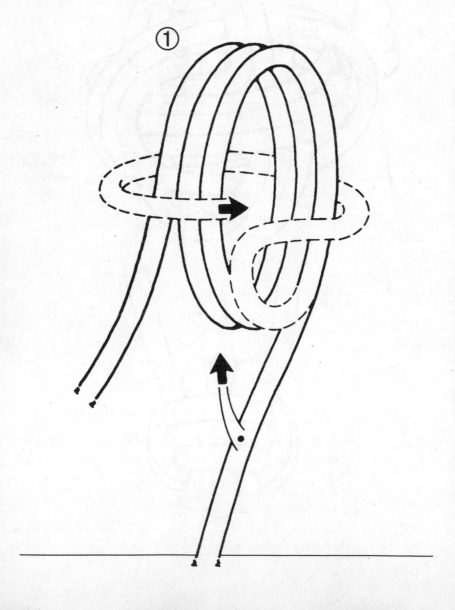

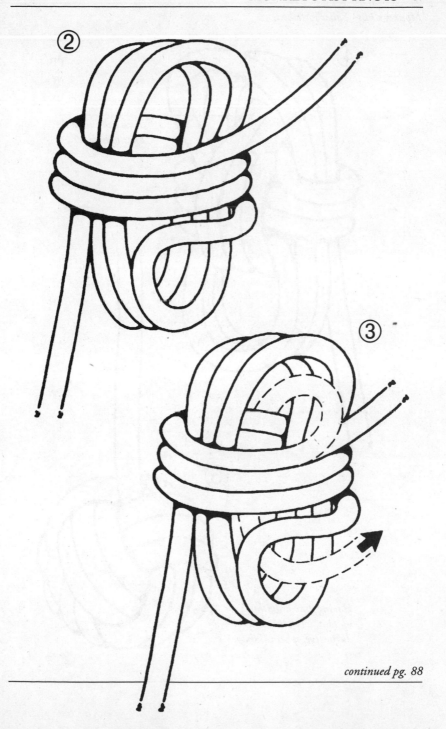

continued pg. 88

Monkey's Fist - Sailor's Method

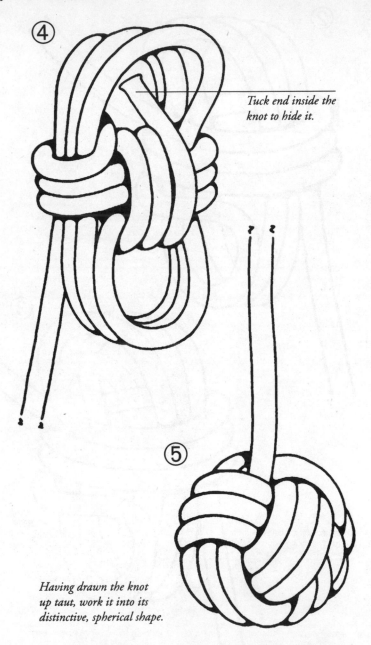

④

Tuck end inside the
knot to hide it.

⑤

Having drawn the knot
up taut, work it into its
distinctive, spherical shape.

5

TURK'S HEAD KNOTS

Turk's Head knots have long been recognized for their highly decorative attributes. Leonardo da Vinci drew them in the fifteenth century and they are still widely used today. They are usually tied around cylindrical objects – in most cases as pure decoration but also to serve many practical purposes from handgrips to napkin rings. There are many recorded variations of these knots, however the examples shown in this chapter are the most common variations whereby the first stages of the knot are constructed around the fingers or in the hand with a single strand of cord or rope, and then placed around a cylindrical object to be completed.

Four Lead, Three Bight Turk's Head

TURK'S HEAD - THREE LEAD, FOUR BIGHT

Single-strand Turk's Head knots are tied by many different methods, producing a wide variety of sizes. The size of this particular knot is "three lead, four bight." The term "lead" refers to a single circuit of the cord around the cylinder or object, and the term "bight" refers to the number of "scallop" shapes formed. The knot is initially formed around the hand as in step 1, then removed to form steps 2, 3 & 4. At this point it is placed around the chosen object to be completed. To create the finished compact knot as in step 6, the slack will need to be worked out. This is done gradually, by starting at one end of the cord and progressing right through the knot to the other end. It may also help to use a pair of thin-nosed pliers.

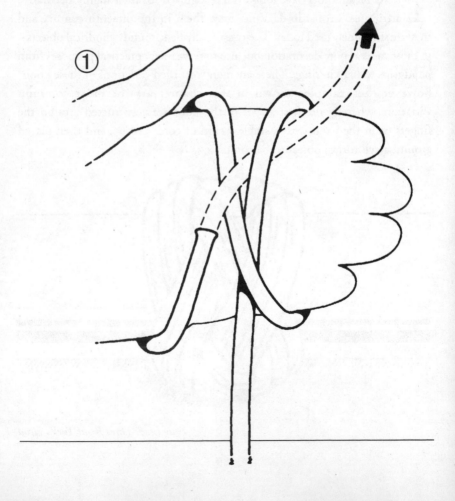

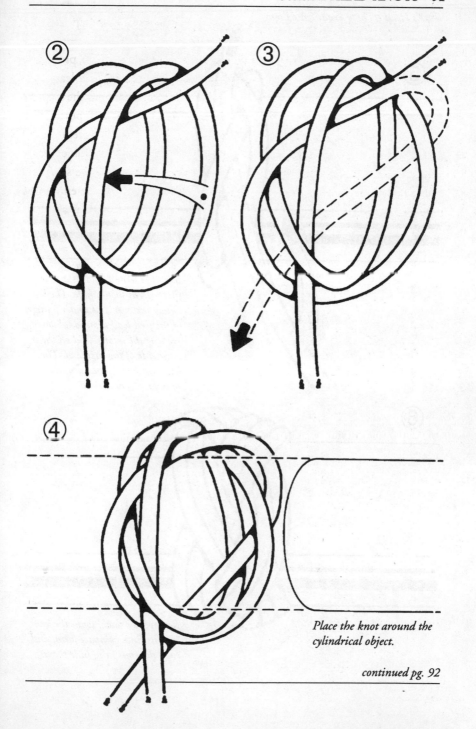

Place the knot around the cylindrical object.

continued pg. 92

Turk's Head - Three Lead, Four Bight

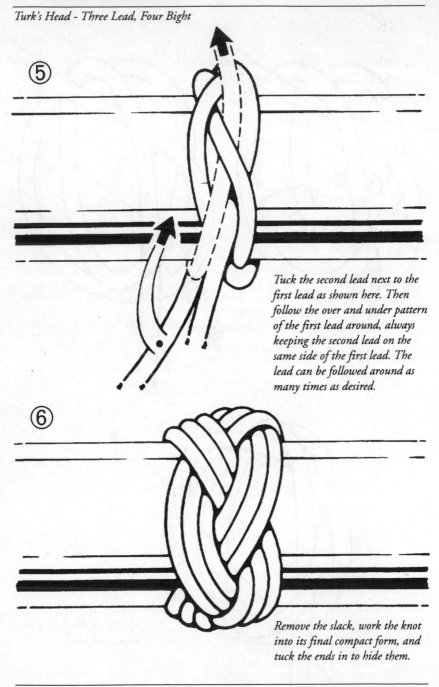

⑤

Tuck the second lead next to the first lead as shown here. Then follow the over and under pattern of the first lead around, always keeping the second lead on the same side of the first lead. The lead can be followed around as many times as desired.

⑥

Remove the slack, work the knot into its final compact form, and tuck the ends in to hide them.

TURK'S HEAD - THREE LEAD, FIVE BIGHT

This method shows how to tie a "three lead, five bight" Turk's Head in a flat form. The knot can be left in this form to create, for example, a mat or drink coaster, or turned down and worked over a cylindrical object to form a decorative covering.

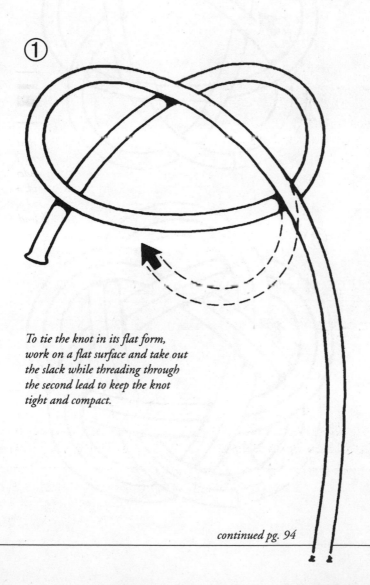

To tie the knot in its flat form, work on a flat surface and take out the slack while threading through the second lead to keep the knot tight and compact.

continued pg. 94

Turk's Head - Three Lead, Five Bight

*The first lead can be followed around by
the second lead as many times as required to
create the finished knot. Always keep the second
lead on the same side of the first lead (the lead
that created the pattern) and tuck the ends
in neatly to hide them.*

TURK'S HEAD - FOUR LEAD, THREE BIGHT

To create step 1 of this "four lead, three bight" version, start as if you are tying a Knife Lanyard Knot (see pg. 44) around the hand. Use the forefinger and thumb as shown in step 2 to create the loose form of the knot before placing it on the chosen object as in step 3. To complete the knot follow the instructions given for the Turk's Head - Three Lead, Four Bight (see pg. 92).

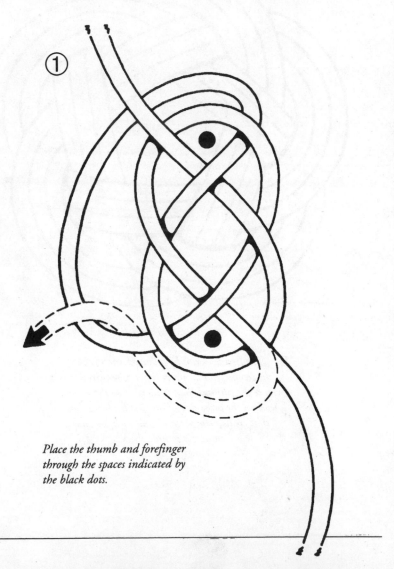

Place the thumb and forefinger through the spaces indicated by the black dots.

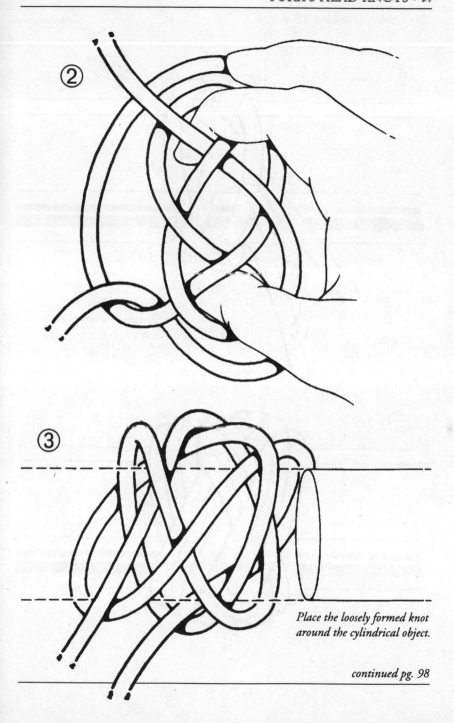

②

③

Place the loosely formed knot around the cylindrical object.

continued pg. 98

Turk's Head - Four Lead, Three Bight

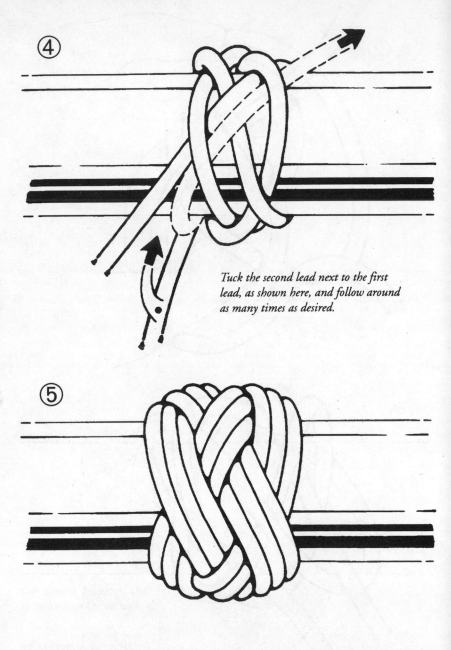

④

Tuck the second lead next to the first lead, as shown here, and follow around as many times as desired.

⑤

6

SINNETS

. . . .

Sinnets are one or more intertwined strands that can be tied from a wide variety of materials. They have a vast range of decorative applications – from belts and bracelets to schoolgirls' pigtails. There are three main types of sinnets: plait or braid sinnets, chain sinnets, and crown sinnets. Within these groups are many variations; this chapter shows some of the most decorative and commonly used examples.

Double Flat Sinnet

Five-Strand Sinnet

FLAT SINNET

This simple, three-strand, plait or braid sinnet is also known as the English or Common Sinnet. It has a vast range of decorative applications, but undoubtedly the most popular is to plait schoolgirls' pigtails. Arrange the three strands as in step 1, (if necessary secure them in a straight line with a clip or simple clamp). The method of tying is to alternately cross the outside strands over the center strand; start with right-hand strand as in step 2, next the left-hand strand as in step 3. Now keep repeating this process as in steps 4 & 5, until you reach the desired length of sinnet. To achieve a neat, compact sinnet as in step 6, tighten and arrange the plait at each step of the tying. Sinnets can be finished off in a variety of ways depending on their final use. The simplest method is by clamping with a thin string, cord, or an elastic band and then trimming off the excess if necessary.

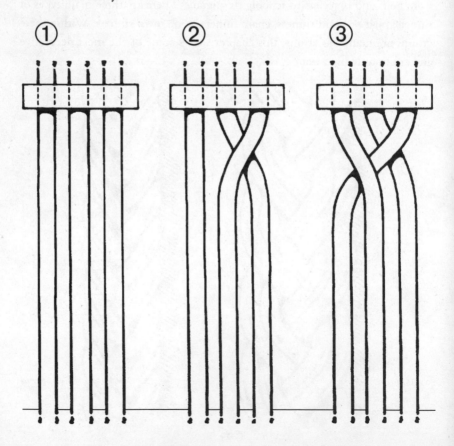

④ ⑤ ⑥

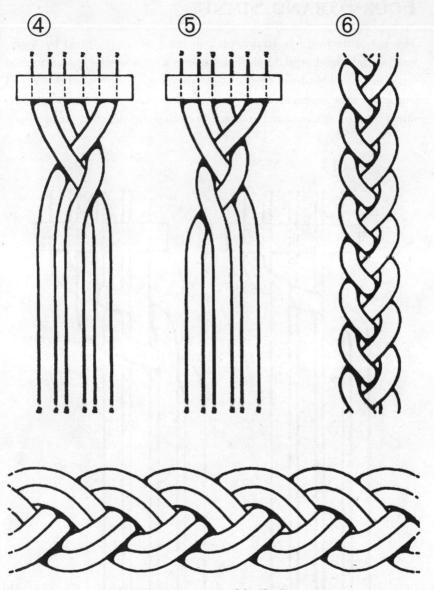

*This attractive variation of the Flat Sinnet is
created by doubling the strands – use
six strands, arranged in three pairs, and follow
exactly the same tying procedure.*

FOUR-STRAND SINNET

This very attractive, four-strand, plait or braid sinnet is created by always weaving the strand on the right-hand side as shown in step 1. Continue to weave only the right-hand strand, as shown in steps 2 & 3, until the desired length of sinnet has been created. To achieve the final result as in step 4, the sinnet must be tightened and arranged at each step of the tying procedure.

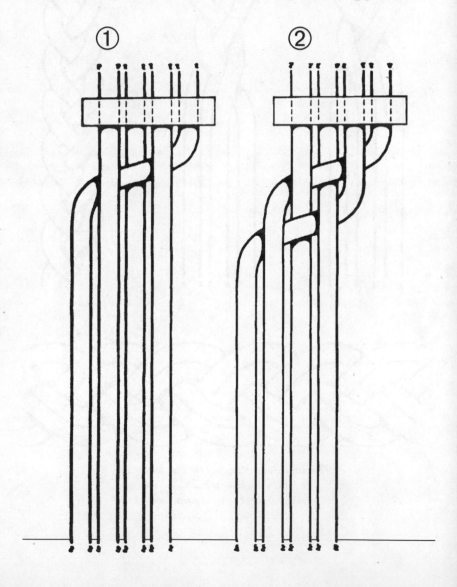

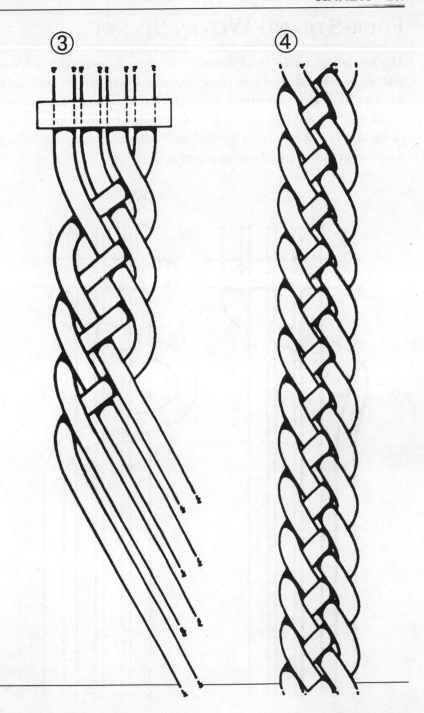

FOUR-STRAND WOVEN SINNET

This four-strand, plait or braid sinnet is an excellent example of the variations that can be achieved. This very ornamental sinnet is created by weaving just one strand through the other three. Arrange the four strands with the right-hand strand woven through as in step 1. Now continue to weave that strand as shown in steps 2 & 3. To create the final result as in step 4, tighten and arrange the sinnet at each step of the tying process.

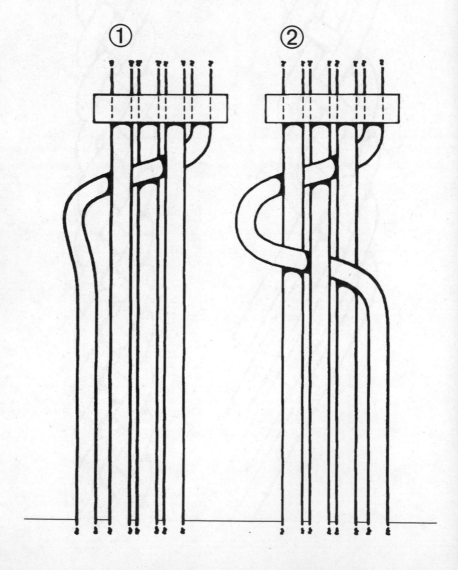

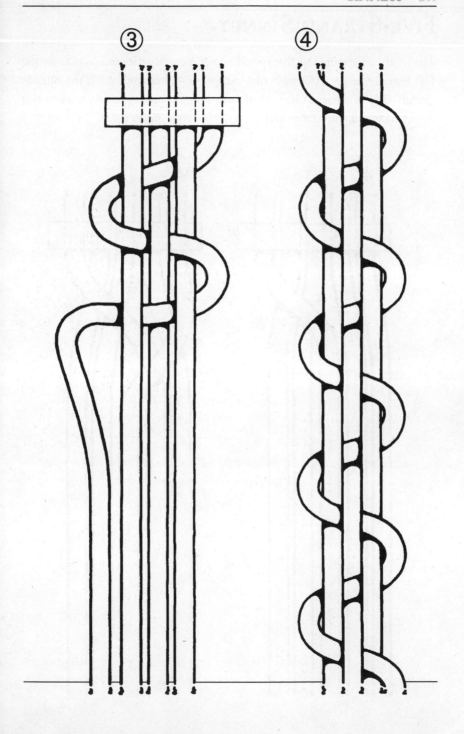

FIVE-STRAND SINNET

The method for tying this five-strand sinnet is exactly the same as that for the Flat Sinnet (see pg. 100) with one exception – alternately cross the outside strands over two strands instead of one. For the best appearance, keep this sinnet tight and compact at each step of the tying procedure.

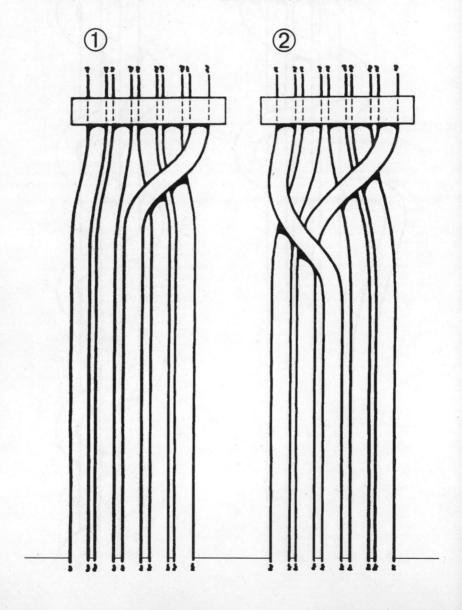

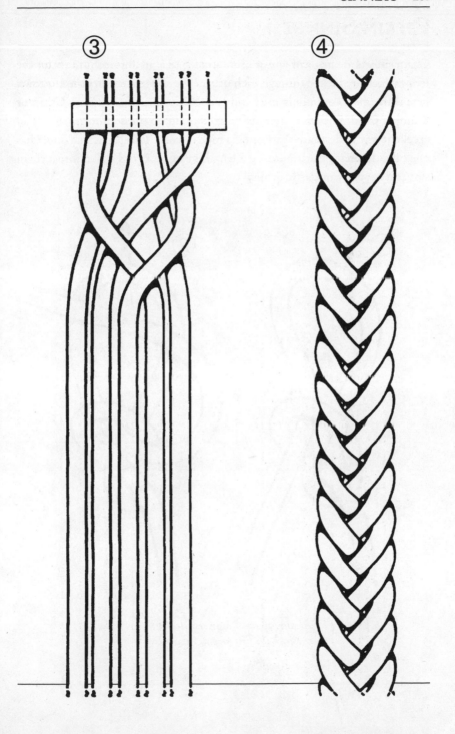

CHAIN SINNET

Chain sinnets are made of one or more strands that are formed into successive loops which are tucked through each other. The single-strand example shown here is the most commonly used and is also known as the Monkey Chain or Trumpet Cord. It is often seen tied in gold braid on dress uniforms and is an excellent way to decoratively shorten a rope or cord. This particular sinnet has one other interesting attribute – if a length of rope or cord is tied into a chain sinnet it acquires an elastic quality.

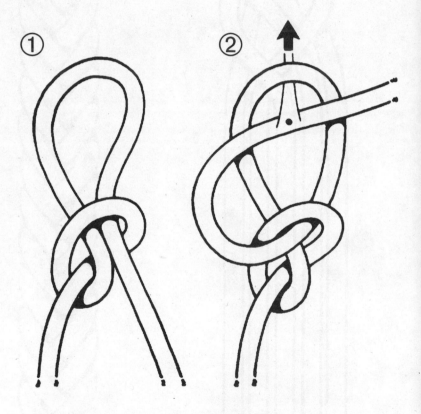

Arrange the cord as in step 1 and then tuck the first loop as in step 2.

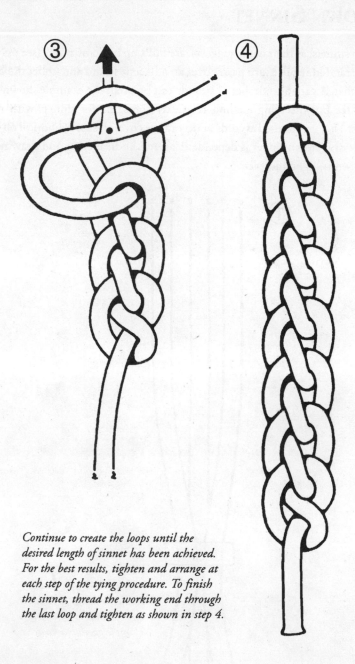

Continue to create the loops until the desired length of sinnet has been achieved. For the best results, tighten and arrange at each step of the tying procedure. To finish the sinnet, thread the working end through the last loop and tighten as shown in step 4.

CROWN SINNET

Crown sinnets, as their name suggests, are built up by "crowning" (see pg. 62). Each strand in regular turn passes over an adjacent strand and under the bight of another. A variable number of strands can be used; the example shown here uses three but the tying method is exactly the same for sinnets with more strands. They can be used as cords or decorative coverings for cylindrical objects. A successful crown sinnet is dependent on methodical tying and drawing up the crowns – tight and even.

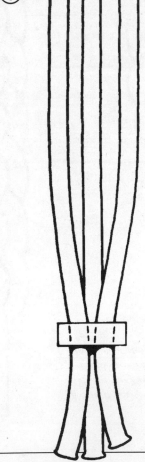

Clamp or tie three strands together with thin cord or an elastic band, or tie all three strands together with a simple overhand knot.

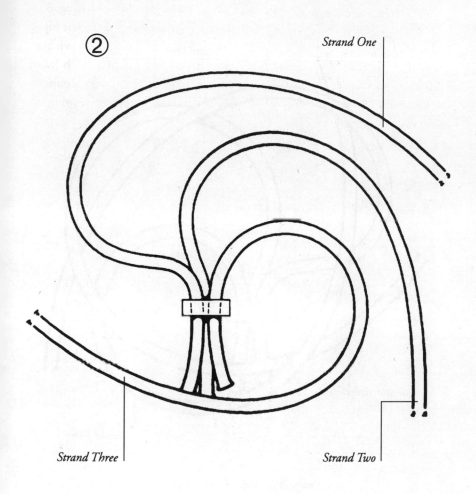

Strand One

Strand Three

Strand Two

*Arrange the three strands like this,
in preparation for crowning to begin.*

continued pg. 112

Crown Sinnet

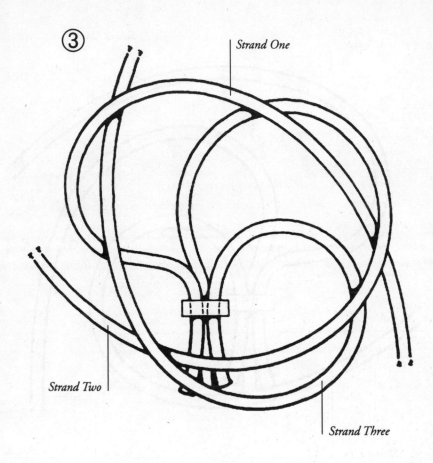

As shown in this illustration, create the first crown by placing strand one over strand two, strand two over strand three, and strand three over and then under strand one. Draw the strands tight and the first crown is formed.

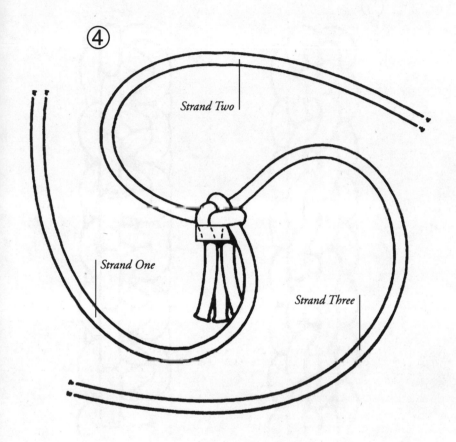

④

Strand Two

Strand One

Strand Three

Now continue to build the sinnet with
successive crowns. To create this particular Crown
Sinnet the crowns must always be worked
in the same direction, in this case, clockwise.

continued pg. 114

Crown Sinnet

⑤

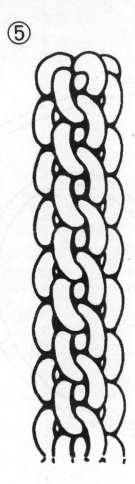

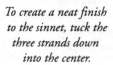

To create a neat finish
to the sinnet, tuck the
three strands down
into the center.

This interesting variation
of the Crown Sinnet is created
by alternating clockwise and
anti-clockwise crowns to form
a triangular-shaped sinnet.

7

FLAT KNOTS

· · · · · · · · · · · · · · · · · · · ·

The highly decorative appearance of flat or two-dimensional knots may look complex, but if the tying instructions are followed correctly they should present no great difficulties. The most common use for this type of knot is as household or marine mats, but they also have a very practical use in protecting objects from wear by rubbing or chafing – as boat fenders for example. To create round matting or drink coasters, use the Turk's Head - Three Lead, Five Bight (see pg. 93) in its flat form.

Ocean Plat

OCEAN PLAT

This classic flat knot is found all over the world in a surprising number of situations – the most common being as a door mat or matting found aboard a ship or boat. The size of the example shown here, which is the one most widely used, is based on three side bights. This pattern can be made more solid by increasing the number of times the lead is followed around, but the actual size of the knot can not be increased. To increase the size of the knot, the number of side bights has to be increased. For example, increase to six or nine bights to create a long, narrow mat or tread for a companionway aboard a ship or boat.

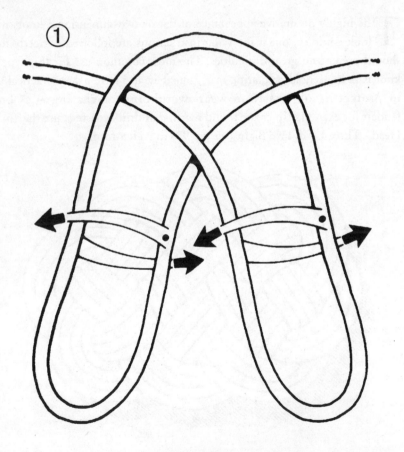

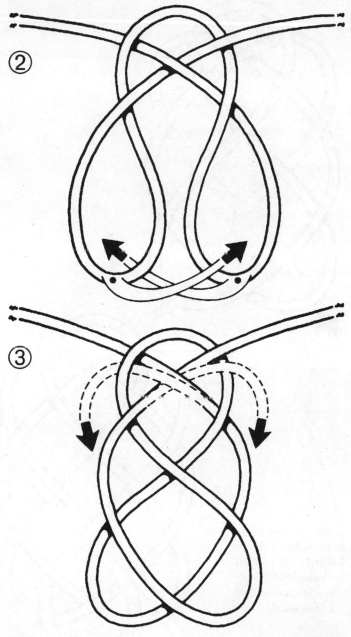

②

③

Continued pg. 118

Ocean Plat

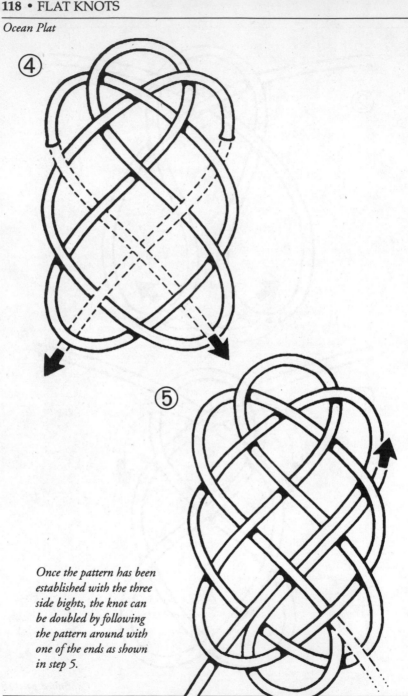

Once the pattern has been established with the three side bights, the knot can be doubled by following the pattern around with one of the ends as shown in step 5.

⑥

The knot can be doubled or followed
around as many times as desired. It can
also be left loosely formed as shown above,
or it can be tightened and made solid
as in step 7.

Continued pg. 120

Ocean Plat

⑦

To finish, hide the ends by tucking them
into the weave on the underside of the knot.
If the knot is to be used as a mat, the whole structure
can be greatly strengthened by sewing together all
of the intersecting points with strong thread.

CHINESE KNOT

This rectangular flat knot is created by enlarging a Carrick Bend Knot. The Carrick Bend is tied using two cords, as in step 1, then gradually enlarged by alternately tucking over and under two diagonally opposite ends across the knot. To add to the already decorative appearance of this knot, the ends can be brought out of the four corners and finished with other decorative knots, for example, Multiple Overhand Knots (see pg. 20), as in step 5.

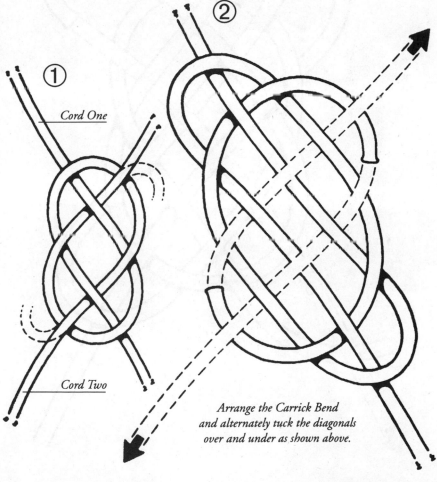

Cord One

Cord Two

Arrange the Carrick Bend and alternately tuck the diagonals over and under as shown above.

Continued pg. 122

Chinese Knot

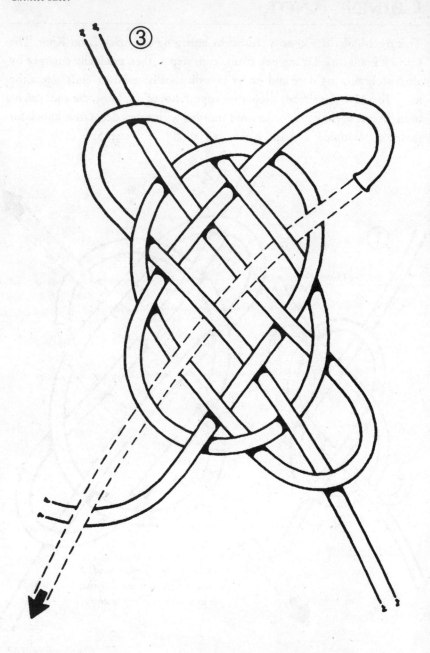

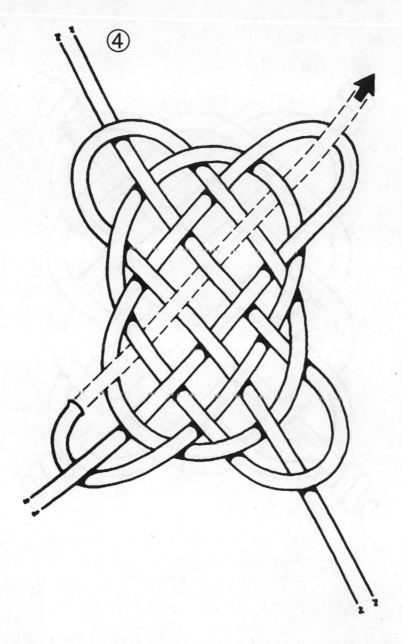

Continued pg. 124

Chinese Knot

⑤

To finish, arrange and work the knot into its final
form and add decorative stopper knots to
the four ends.

8

APPLIED
DECORATIVE KNOTS

. . . .

Decorative knots can be used individually or in elaborate combinations; they can be used for practical purposes or pure decoration. This chapter shows just a few examples of how to use decorative knots, but remember with the information contained in this book and a little imagination the possibilities are endless!

A Turk's Head Curtain Tieback

DECORATIVE BUTTONS

To further enhance the decorative appearance of Button Knots (see pg. 69), they can be attached to garments by using flat appliquéd knots known as "frogs." Each button is attached using two frogs – one creates a loop for the button hole and the other secures the button knot itself. The Turk's Head - Three Lead, Five Bight (see pg. 93) in its flat form would make a suitable frog, but increasing it to a seven bight knot, as illustrated here in steps 1, 2 and 3, gives it a more circular and decorative appearance. The finished assembly of two frogs and a Double Chinese Button Knot (see pg. 72) is shown in step 5.

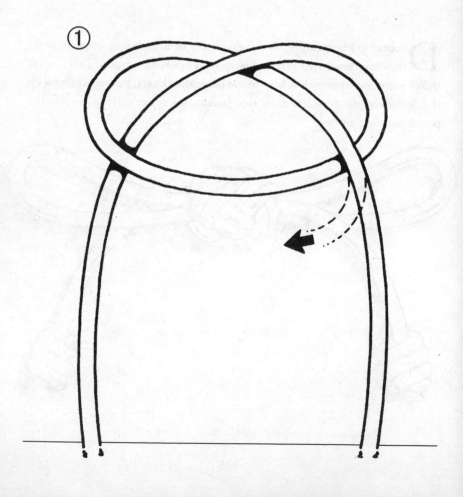

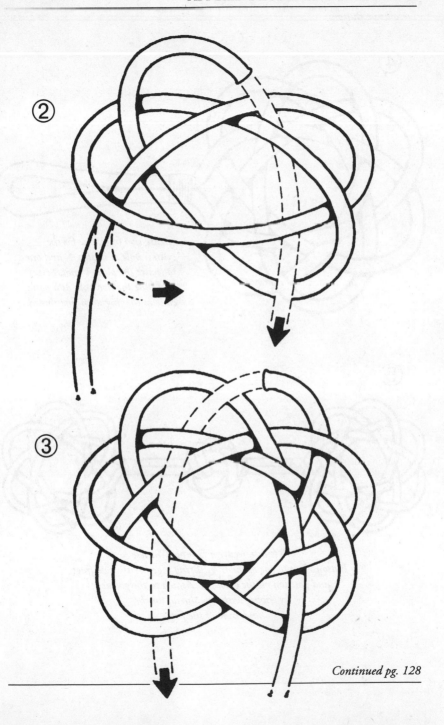

Continued pg. 128

Decorative Buttons

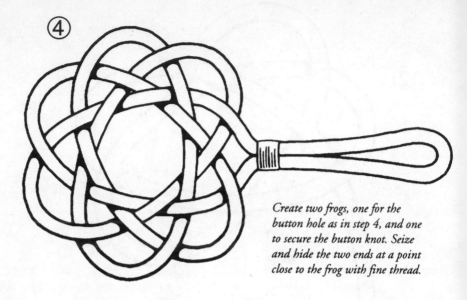

Create two frogs, one for the
button hole as in step 4, and one
to secure the button knot. Seize
and hide the two ends at a point
close to the frog with fine thread.

To finish, secure a Double Chinese
Button Knot to one of the frogs. Bring together the two frogs
and position on the garment. Attach to the garment
by sewing with fine thread on the
underside of the frogs.

TURK'S HEAD CURTAIN TIEBACK

Expensive looking curtain tiebacks are surprisingly easy to make. Arrange a length of high quality cord, as in step 1, and seize it in the center with tape or thread as shown. Now, with a second piece of cord, tie a snug-fitting Turk's Head - Four Lead, Three Bight (see pg. 96) around the first piece of cord covering the seized area. To finish, as in step 2, tie the two ends with Multiple Overhand Knots (see pg. 20).

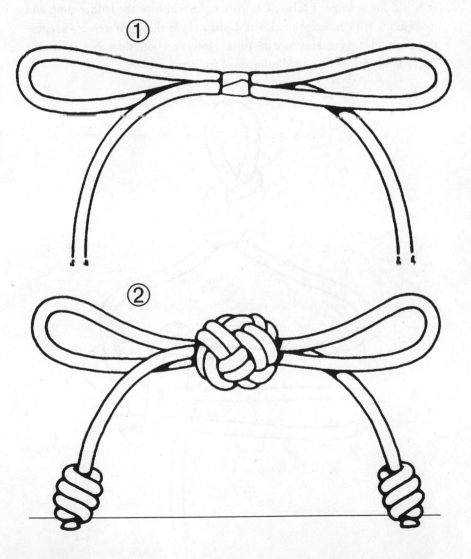

ROPE LADDER

This is a fine example of how decorative knotting can create an extremely useful piece of equipment. To tie a ladder of any substantial size is going to require a long length of rope, so provision for this should be made before starting. To start, take a length of rope, middle it, and tie a loop in the bight of the rope. In the example shown here, a Figure-Eight Loop has been used. Arrange the left end as in step 1, and pass the right end through, as shown, to start making a series of turns. Determine the width of the ladder rung and make as many turns as required. Finish the rung as shown in step 2 – keeping the turns tight and making sure the rung is secure on both sides. Now continue the process until the required number of rungs are achieved.

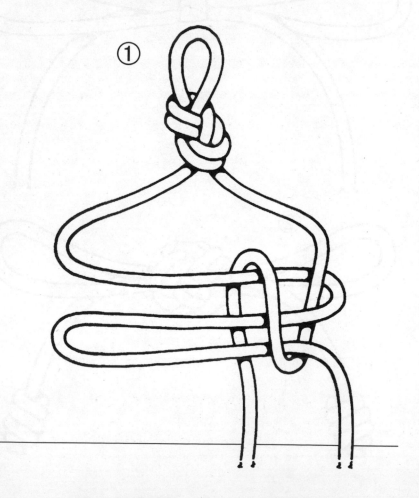

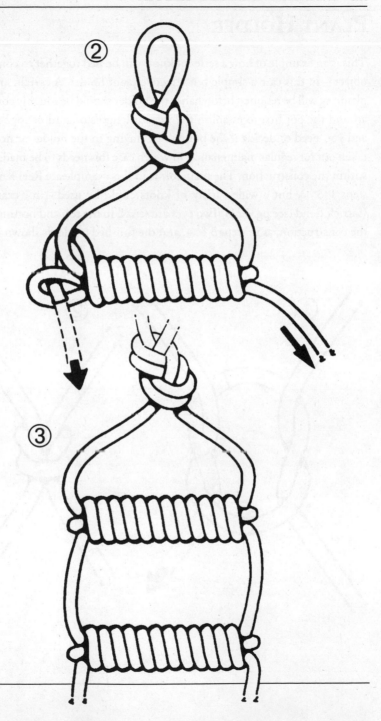

PLANT HOLDER

This is an example of how a series of knots can be tied together to construct an object – in this case a simple but effective plant holder. A certain amount of planning will be required beforehand; the holder should be roughly constructed around the pot first to establish the various lengths of cord or rope required, and you need to decide if the pot will be staying in the holder or needs to be taken out for regular maintenance, in which case this needs to be made possible within the construction. The main joints in this example are Reef Knots, as in steps 1 & 2, but a wide variety of knots could be used – for example the Carrick Bend (see pg. 121). Two eyes are seized in the top and bottom parts of the construction, as in steps 3 & 4, and the finished holder is shown in step 5.

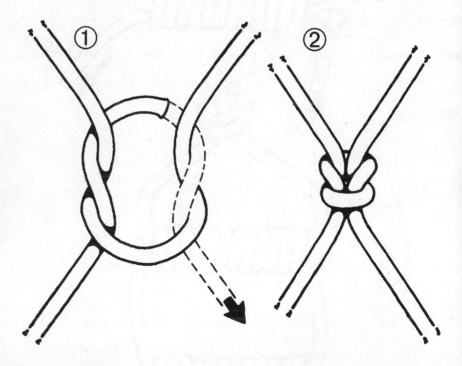

③ ④

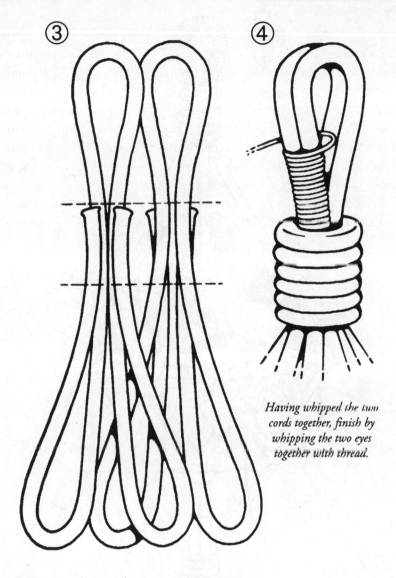

Having whipped the two cords together, finish by whipping the two eyes together with thread.

To create the top or bottom section, arrange two lengths of cord as above, and seize them together as shown in step 4, by using the same technique as shown on page 16 for whipping the end of a rope.

Continued pg. 134

Plant Holder

⑤

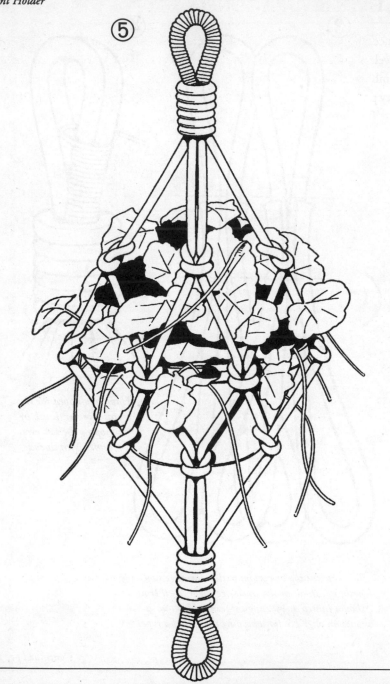

CHINESE DRAGONFLY

Since the mid-nineteenth century there has been a fascination, especially by jewelers, with creating the shapes of insects and butterflies by using various combinations of decorative knots. This Chinese Dragonfly has proved to be a very popular example; it is made up of a Chinese Button Knot (see pg. 70) and two True-Lover's Knots (see pg. 58).

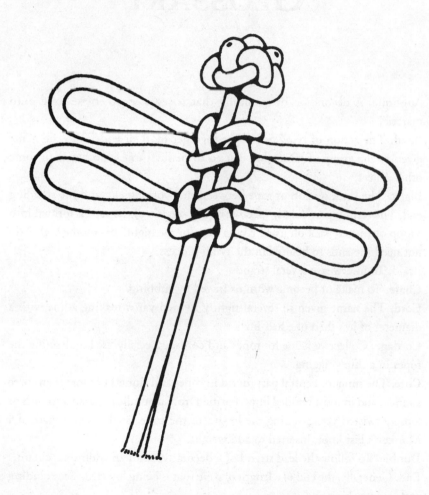

GLOSSARY

· · · · · · · · · · · · · · · · ·

Appliqué. A decoration or trimming that is sewn or otherwise fixed onto material.

Bend. The action of tying two ropes together by their ends. Also the name given to the group of knots that is used to tie lines to each other or to some other object.

Bight. The slack section of rope between the working end and the standing end. The term is particularly used when this section of the rope is formed into a loop or turned back on itself. Knots tied "in the bight" or "on the bight" do not need the ends to be used in the tying process.

Braid. To interweave several strands.

Chafe. To make or become worn or frayed by rubbing.

Cord. The name given to several tightly twisted yarns making a line with a diameter of less than one half-inch.

Cordage. Collective name for ropes and cords, especially used to describe the ropes in a ship's rigging.

Core. The inner or central part found in ropes and sinnets of more than three strands, and in most braided lines. Formed from a bundle of parallel strands or loosely twisted yarn running the length of the rope, or the central part of a Monkey's Fist knot, inserted to add weight.

Double. To follow the lead strand of a decorative knot an additional circuit.

End. Generally, the end of a length of rope that is being knotted. See **standing end** and **working end**.

Eye. Loop formed at the end of a length of rope by seizing.

Fancy Knot. Any decorative knot including ones that have a practical use.

Fender. A cushion of flexible material, positioned on the sides of boats to prevent damage when tying up or mooring.

Finish. To add the final touches or to make the final arrangement.

Follow the lead. To pass a cord along a path parallel to the first lead strand, usually in an over and under movement.

Fray. To unravel, especially the end of a piece of rope.

Frog. A flat appliquéd knot that is sewn or otherwise attached to garments or uniforms. Serves the purpose of securing a button knot and providing the button hole.

Heaving line. A line with a weighted knot tied at one end, that is attached to another heavier line and is thrown from boat to shore or to another vessel. The purpose of the heaving line is to draw behind it a heavier line that will be used for tying up or mooring.

Lanyard. A short length of rope or cord made decorative with knots and sinnets. Used to secure personal objects; usually worn around the neck or attached to a belt.

Lay. The direction, right or left-handed, of the twist in the strands that form a rope.

Lead. The direction the working end takes through a knot. When a knot is doubled, the lead is followed around by the working end for a second time.

Line. Generic name for cordage with no specific purpose, although it can describe a particular use (clothes line, fishing line, etc.).

Loop. Part of a rope that is bent so that it comes together across itself.

Middle (To). To establish the center of a piece of rope or cord by laying the two ends together.

Over and under. Description of the weave in knots such as the Turk's Head.

Plain-laid rope. Three-stranded rope laid (twisted) to the right.

Plait or Plat. Pronounced *plat*. To intertwine strands in a pattern.

Rope. Strong, thick cord more than one inch in circumference and made from twisted strands of fiber, wire, etc.

Rung. The crosspiece that forms a step of a ladder.

Seizing. To bind two cords or ropes together.

Sinnet or **Sennet.** Braided cordage (flat, round, or square), formed from three to nine cords.

S-laid rope. Left-hand-laid rope.

Small stuff. Thin cordage, twine, string, rope, or line that has a circumference of less than one inch, or a diameter of less than one half-inch.

Standing end. The short area at the end of the standing part of the rope.

Standing part. The part of the rope that is fixed and under tension (as opposed to the free working end with which the knot is tied).

Stopper knot. Any terminal knot used to bind the end of a line, cord, or rope to prevent it from unravelling and also to provide a decorative end.

Strand. Yarns twisted together in the opposite direction to the yarn itself. Rope made from strands (rope that is not braided) is called laid line.

Taut. Tightly stretched.

Thread. A fine cord of twisted filaments - especially of cotton - used in sewing and weaving.

Whipping. Tightly wrapping small stuff around the end of a cord or rope to prevent it from fraying.

Work (To). To draw up and shape a knot; to make the final arrangement.

Working end. The part of the cord or rope used actively in tying a knot. The opposite of the **standing end.**

Yarn. The basic element of a cord or rope formed from synthetic filaments or natural fibers.

Z-laid rope. Right-hand-laid rope.

INDEX OF KNOTS

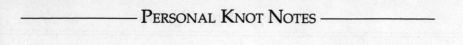